SEEING THROUGH THE GLASS DARKLY

Bullying, Racism, Prejudice,
Topped with the Fairy DNA Cherry

JOHN — Cousin
GARLICK

The opinions expressed in this manuscript are solely the opinions of the author and do not represent the opinions or thoughts of the publisher. The author has represented and warranted full ownership and/or legal right to publish all the materials in this book.

Seeing Through the Glass Darkly
Bullying, Racism, Prejudice, Topped with the Fairy DNA Cherry
All Rights Reserved.
Copyright © 2013 John Garlick
v2.0

Cover Photo © 2013 JupiterImages Corporation. All rights reserved - used with permission.

This book may not be reproduced, transmitted, or stored in whole or in part by any means, including graphic, electronic, or mechanical without the express written consent of the publisher except in the case of brief quotations embodied in critical articles and reviews.

Outskirts Press, Inc.
http://www.outskirtspress.com

ISBN: 978-1-4787-0784-4

Outskirts Press and the "OP" logo are trademarks belonging to Outskirts Press, Inc.

PRINTED IN THE UNITED STATES OF AMERICA

Contents

Chapter 1:   Let Me Introduce Myself 1

Chapter 2:   My Early Years 7

Chapter 3:   The Changing Wind 16

Chapter 4:   A Kid Becoming a Man 20

Chapter 5:   It Will Get Better 29

Chapter 6:   The Wonder Years 34

Chapter 7:   Winding It Down 38

Chapter 8:   Free at Last, Free at Last 42

Chapter 9:   Back Home 45

Chapter 10: The Best Summer Ever 48

Chapter 11: It's Raining Again 57

Chapter 12: Now It's Pouring 61

Chapter 13: Life Goes On 67

Chapter 14: Another Life 73

Chapter 15: Right Here Waiting for You 81

Chapter 16: Happy Birthday Johnny 86

Chapter 17: Promises Not Kept 89

Chapter 18: And So It Goes 94

Chapter 19: The Battle for Jessica 100

Chapter 20: Game of Volleyball, Anyone? 103

Chapter 21: My Tribe to the Rescue 106

Chapter 22: Drowning or Murder? 109

Chapter 23: Good Things Come to Those Who Weight 121

Chapter 24: I Need a Break! 124

Chapter 25: What Have I Done? 127

Chapter 26: The Worst Mistake of All 134

Chapter 27: Follow the Yellow Brick Road to the Emerald City 137

Chapter 28: Like a Kid in a Candy Store 140

Chapter 29: Do You Need Help? 145

Chapter 30: The Years with Ken 155

Chapter 31: Breaking Up Is So Hard to Do 163

Chapter 32: Goodbye Capitol Hill, Hello Central District 169

Chapter 33: To the Platform of Deliverance 173

Chapter 34: Close the Beacons of Your Mind,
Clear Your Love, Cut the Cord 177

Chapter 35: So Long to Our Love 180

Chapter 36: Reunited 188

Chapter 37: Emptiness 193

Chapter 38: Final Goodbye 200

Chapter 39: The Autumn of 2009 203

Chapter 40: Thanks for the Trips, Ken 211

Chapter 41: Off to a New Beginning 213

CHAPTER 1

Let Me Introduce Myself

BEING BORN A mixture of part Irish, Native American Indian, and Canadian-French was a great beginning for a recipe of an alcoholic. My family's history could attest to that fact, so throughout my life I have been very careful not to put that recipe to the test. Added to that recipe was a dash of Fairy DNA, giving me the gay gene—butch, thankfully.

The early morning hours of September 19, 1957 bore witness to the addition of a gay Indian to Lewistown, Montana, population 8000. Since I had been born to a registered member of the Turtle Mountain Chippewa Tribe, I believe my mom wanted to give me an Indian name, so Coyote was Mom's first choice. My mother was Metis, three-quarters Chippewa and one quarter Canadian-French, and she loved coyotes. She had tried unsuccessfully during her childhood, in Roy, Montana, to raise coyote pups as the persistent and hopeful might tame dogs on their ranches. My grandmother would always tell her that coyotes could not be domesticated; they were born wild and to the wild they would return. But that never stopped my mother from trying. I guess she had to try one more time, time and again, holding on to something she truly loved and wanted to share with me, her youngest of six and last child. I guess it wouldn't have been too bad—carrying the moniker "Coyote," could have built character in me, like Johnny Cash's "A Boy Named Sue." Dad put the kibosh on that selection, pointing out that other kids might not see "Coyote" as endearing as Mom saw it. Culture was one thing. The realities of growing up in rural Montana were quite another.

Mom's second choice was Jesse James. Now we're talking. I would have loved it. It would have had a certain charisma to it, a certain coolness and bravado. Gay, butch, bullseye. Perhaps Mom knew even at birth that I was "different" from her other children? I would like to think so, but since I will never really know, it is a fantasy I have always enjoyed. But again, Dad overruled that name, citing again that other children would use it against me, make my life a little bit harder. If Dad had only known what was in store for me, I think Coyote or Jesse James would have gotten a free pass.

September, my birth month, would come to be my favorite month of the year. Not because my birthday was in that month, but because of the Indian summers that were so astonishing in Montana. The hot days of summer were over, but winter had not yet gripped us in his frigid hands. There was that crispness in the morning air, warming to a pleasant temperature in the afternoon, and an even more perfect evening, ending a perfect day.

So I was given the name John Edward Garlick, borrowing the names from my two uncles on my mom's side. A proper and dignified name, it has grounded me to both sides of my family, the LaFountains and the Garlicks.

My father, Emery Lawrence Garlick, was forty-two when I was born. He was of Irish descent, was handsome and one hell of a tap dancer. His mother had died while he was a baby and his father abandoned the family, running off with the carnival, taking his oldest brother with him, leaving the responsibility of raising the other four children to his sister. Dad never took us to the carnival when it came to town, as he could not tolerate the carnival people—traveling trauma makes a stop in Lewistown. I guess it made him think of his father deserting him. Dad was a laborer at the Montana Lumber Yard approximately two blocks from our Lewistown home

Dad was both gentle and strong. He wanted me to be involved

LET ME INTRODUCE MYSELF

in sports and I suppose was disappointed when I showed no interest, but we bonded in other ways. Dad instilled in me my love of plants and gardening. Every spring, Dad and I would plan where and what we were going to plant in the garden. I would get so excited and Dad would harness that excitement and channel my energy into producing a beautiful garden every year. Besides the "standards," he would always give me my choice of planting pumpkins, gourds, sunflowers, or whatever I was enchanted with each year. He never questioned my choices and taught me the craft of tending and caring for something living.

I remember a year we had a very late frost and Dad woke me before the sun had risen and told me what had happened. I was devastated. Everything had germinated and was growing. He told me that we were going to save the garden; he was going to show me how. I was curious, but doubt never entered my mind. We went out and I found the garden covered in a blanket of white. It was a hard frost and my heart sank. Dad told me to get the garden hose and turn the water on. I returned with the nozzle turned to the spray dial. Dad took the hose and started spraying the water on the frozen landscape. He explained that as long as we melted the frost away before the sun's rays hit it, no permanent damage would be done to the plants. He handed the hose to me and I took over spraying. He wanted me to share in saving the garden, and save it we did. It flourished. This was one of so many lessons in life that Dad passed on to me. Another thing we shared was tools. When it came to building, Dad was very handy. Was he a great carpenter? No, but he taught me enough to be my own handyman in my home today. He showed me how to not hit my thumb with the hammer. My father provided for his family both financially and emotionally. I was a very lucky son.

My mother, Dorothy LaFountain, was thirty-eight at the time of my birth. Her mother was born in a teepee in North Dakota. We are known as the Landless Indians, as we are the only tribe that never received land from the US government, as they paid us approximately ten cents an acre for the land we had, which included parts of

◄ SEEING THROUGH THE GLASS DARKLY

Wisconsin, Minnesota, Michigan, Lake Superior, Lake Huron, and later parts of the Dakotas and Montana. The total settlement was one million dollars for 9,000,000 acres ceded to the US government. Our tribe was the Turtle Mountain Band, so called as our people came from the Turtle Mountains, the area of north central North Dakota and southwestern Manitoba.

My people loved this area and wanted the Feds to give us this land as our reservation. The government would not, branding us with the term the "Landless Indians" and the infamous "Ten Cents Treaty." The government later provided in 1892 for approximately two townships within the Turtle Mountain area to act as a reservation. My entire family partook in that ten cents settlement in the 1970s, almost a century after its signing. Some members of my family from the LaFountain side still carry resentment toward the government for what they did to our heritage and birthright. I view it as "survival of the fittest." This happens to cultures all over the world. We were no different. Not right, but just the way it is. Can't be angry forever, this is who we are as the human race. Resentment, I have learned can be a critical part of the recipe to becoming an alcoholic. This anger should certainly not be an excuse to be a drunken Indian, something I disdain—a view that my friends are surprised and sometimes offended by, but then again they are "my people" and I say this as a critique, not as a slur against my heritage. I grew up with this behavior and therefore my description may not be politically correct, but it is accurate, much the same when blacks use the word "nigger." African-Americans at times seem to use it as a term of endearment. I do not like the term "nigger," but I do understand that it is so historically charged and horrible that nobody can blame blacks for using the word in any way they choose. Again I feel I am entitled to make politically incorrect observations about my tribe because they are "my people," and I have the right to express my disfavor with this kind of behavior among my Indian ancestry.

My mother never used her middle name, would never tell me what it was, and just said she hated it. I guess she really did, as I never found out what it was. My mother was a petite woman, strikingly beautiful: high cheekbones, perfect white teeth, black hair with a purple hue, and a very narrow waistline. She was the matriarch of the family, and my father, being the gentle soul he was, conceded that role to her, and it worked out for the benefit of the family. My mother was very strong-willed and very opinionated. She was also very family-oriented and very conscious of right and wrong. Having grown up with an alcoholic father, she would relate to us, her children, stories of my grandfather bringing a loaded gun to her parents' bed, threatening to kill the entire family before sunrise. Such trauma left a scar on my mother that she kept with her until death. My mother could not tolerate drinking in our home life, which caused a few ugly fights between my mom and dad while I was growing up. The few times my dad did drink and Mom would find out, we would have front row seats to Mom screaming and throwing dishes at Dad, who generally was able to evade the incoming shells. My parents were very passionate, and I guess that is why they stayed together until my father passed away in 1984. There is something to be said for passion, right?

One of my fondest and earliest memories of my mother was her chasing me around the swing set. I obviously had done something wrong and Mom was going to give me the punishment I deserved, but first she had to catch me. I was probably two or three at the time and I remember going around and around the swing set with Mom on my heels. It must have been a Sunday, as Dad was home, the only day he had off from his work week, and he was laughing at the both of us. Mom was yelling at me to stop, yelling at Dad to stop me. Dad let the drama play out and soon Mom was laughing as she was chasing me calling me a "little shit." She eventually caught me and I was annoyed because I had not "won." Mom told me if I was going to act like a baby, I should be treated as such. She then proceeded to pull her breast out from her dress and tried to make me suck her nipple, which I resisted, but Mom eventually won. I tried pulling away, but Mom held me tighter and gently rocked me until I calmed down. Years later I would relate this story to my first partner Ken, who was a psychologist. He was very impressed with how my mother handled the situation, "pulling" me in with love instead of "pushing" me away with anger.

The people who know me the best will say that I am passionate in many facets of life. I can exaggerate to the point of being a drama queen, always with good intentions. This I owe to my parents. From the positive to the negative, the good and bad, the yin and yang, they taught me both sides.

CHAPTER 2

My Early Years

MY EARLY CHILDHOOD years were very good. Being the youngest of six children, I guess I was spoiled, but I never really thought much about it; I was too busy getting what I wanted, when I wanted it.

There was a nineteen-year age difference between myself and my oldest brother, Marvin. We were more like acquaintances rather than siblings. He was very pro-military, belonged to the Army Reserves, owned many guns, and was very "red state" in his political views, the exact opposite of myself—gay Montana liberals...you could fit all of us in a large sedan.

My second oldest brother, Leland, was eighteen years my senior. Again pretty much like Marvin, except for the military service.

My oldest sister was Patty, nine years my elder. Being closer in age, we had more in common, including political views, and were more like brother and sister.

My brother Billy was seven years older than myself. He was born with CP (cerebral palsy) and was mentally retarded. My mother cared for him his entire life and because of his condition he touched my heart and gave me compassion for those who are short-changed in life through no fault of their own. My mother looked for help everywhere and anywhere...anything that might help my brother lead a more normal life. Being raised a Catholic, it did not set well with the Fathers of the Church when my mom and grandma started going to other churches in search of a possible "healing through faith" or any other "cure" that might be out there. I remember Father Donavan telling my mother that it was her fault that Billy was born the way he was because Mom had stepped on a grave and it was God's punishment and that Mom would go to Hell. My mother did not get visibly upset. She stood up and told Father Donavan that what he said might be true, but she would make sure she opened the gate up for him when he arrived in Hell behind her.

I always cringed in school when the developmentally disabled were made fun of and were referred to as "retards." I would be silent and wished I had the courage to say something intelligent or brave to those assholes, who always seemed to be the most popular kids or best-looking in school. I felt shame for not having the courage to act differently. I felt I was the same as those assholes making fun of my brother, just doing it in silence.

From about the age of eleven to his death, I helped my mom more and more with Billy. He was bedridden and would have to be turned periodically so bed sores would not form. He would also have to be carried to the toilet in his later years due to strokes that left him unable to walk. My assistance generally kicked in after school, providing Mom with some respite. My dad was pretty much the cook of the house, and what a great cook he was. My favorite was his dumplings and noodles. His menus consisted of many Irish dishes, a fact lost on me as a child. He would often make us fudge as a treat at night while we studied or watched television.

My parents received much help for Billy from the local Shriners. He needed specialized medical care not exactly available in rural Montana, so the Shriners flew him and my mother to Spokane, Washington. My brother had to stay there for an extended period, so Mom would fly out to Spokane to be with him on weekends. This was all at the expense of the Shriners' Club. To this day, when I see an advertisement on TV for the Shriners' Club, I think back to what they did for my family, and in my heart I am very grateful for their compassion and generosity.

MY EARLY YEARS

Billy died of pneumonia at the age of twenty-two. I was fifteen at the time of his death, which affected my parents deeply and almost caused my father's death. My father was still recovering from a massive heart attack two years earlier and Billy's death landed him in the hospital due to grief and yet another broken heart.

Mary Rose, two years my senior, was named after my grandmother on my mom's side. Early in her life, my brother Leland gave her the nickname "Colonel," which we spelled as "Kernal." Mary was a tomboy, regimented, almost military-like, dating to my earliest memories of her. Everyone except me referred to her as Kernal. I always called her Mary. We were two years apart and I guess out of all my siblings I was the closest to her, which meant, of course, that she would terrorize me at home, typically dominating. We could frequently be found doing the cruel and adversarial things a brother and sister do to each other.

At school it was a different story. No one touched me. They knew better. They would have to deal with my bodyguard and protector, Mary. If I had a problem and someone was picking on me, I would go to her, problem solved. I remember in fourth grade going to her about someone picking on me. She said she would take care of it, but she stated: "Johnny, you have to start acting different. People pick on you because of the way you act, how you talk." I remember not answering her, just putting her response in the very back corner of my mind. I suppose that being "butch" today does not undo the fact that my voice once had hints of Liberace and a multicultural accent in rural Montana. The next year Mary entered junior high school and I was on my own. Her words and wisdom were now my internal bodyguards. I knew I had to survive the remainder of my school years without her. I became very guarded and shy, contemplating her warning, wondering and questioning exactly what those words meant that she offered as advice. Act different. Talk different. Impending doom would have consumed me had I had the foresight to understand her cautions.

Our maternal grandmother lived with us until her passing in May of 1962. I was five when she died; she was ninety-five. "Grandma" would speak to me in Chippewa and old French. At times, she would have her friends over who also spoke in Chippewa and the old French dialect. My parents would speak to us in English. When I entered school, I had a heavy accent and I rolled my r's. By the time first grade started, my teacher was having a very hard time understanding me. It came to a head when this boy cut in front of me at the water fountain and I proceeded to tell him it was unfair. His heavy build was matched only by the nonexistence of any semblance of common decency. His response to my complaint was to turn around, laugh, and then burp in my face. The laughing in my face I would have ignored. But that belch—it smelled so foul I almost threw up; I immediately went to our teacher. I tried explaining what had happened, trying at the same time not to vomit, as the smell was still with me.

My teacher, Miss Landsberry, could not understand what I was trying to say. The word "burp" was getting twisted in my mouth with that "r" in the word. The more I tried to explain and say the word "burp," the more flustered I became, and the more flustered Miss Landsberry became. She would try to pronounce "burp" very slowly, like it was a foreign language she had never heard before, trying to uncover the hidden message I was trying to convey to her. We both got in trouble and my parents were contacted about my "speech problem." They put my sister Mary and me in speech therapy for three years. They scrubbed us of our Chippewa and French, taught us how to correctly swallow with correct tongue placement, and worked hard with me on words with an "oi" configuration, such as "oil" and "oink." We were being fashioned into Wonder Bread. What a loss and lack of cultural competence…but Lewistown was very homogeneous; Indians were dirty and third-rate citizens; there should be no trace of any evidence to indicate they were still in the town. Even our cemetery was segregated for the Indians until the Catholic Church took over that land.

My family was poor and white trash; maybe I should say red trash? But yet our parents provided us with everything we needed to live a full life. We would alternate between having mush or milk toast for supper weeks on end to having half a beef fill our freezer

MY EARLY YEARS

in the fall when we could afford it. We always had fresh vegetables during the summer and fall, and canned like crazy to get us through the winter months. Dad kept to Sundays off and Mom cared for us children, especially for Billy. Our house was typically full of extended family. Aunts, uncles, and cousins were the norm for us, and I grew up thinking it was the norm for everyone. Not until I was invited to a sleepover with my friend Carl did I learn otherwise.

One Friday night I went over to his house and we sat down for supper. There were Carl and his parents. I politely asked where the rest of the family was and his mother seemed perturbed with my question, asking me what I meant by that—awkward! I don't remember how I responded, but I would never ask that question again. At times there might be ten people at our house for supper. As you have guessed by now, lunch was referred to as dinner and dinner was referred to as supper—prairie remnants. This extended family gathering was inviting, comfortable, and I felt secure in this environment. No need for a bodyguard here.

Our education was very important to my mother, who never attended high school. Her father had lost the family ranch through gambling and drinking, forcing Mom to start working around the age of twelve. My mother strongly encouraged all of her children to finish high school. She was successful with that goal only with her last two children.

"LaFountain" was a name that was not looked upon with much respect in Lewistown; Indian decent, strike one. LaFountains were known as drunks, strike two; and lastly as drug dealers, strike three. Most of that was true, but on the flip side we certainly had our good points. We were a happy, big-hearted people, as most Indians I know are. We had our brushes with the law, family services, and various businesses, but yet down deep we were a good people. One would just have to dig through the shit that frequently buried us to find our true nature—the hidden pony in the pile of shit.

I remember my cousin, Doris; a simple woman, unpretentious, and by all accounts, a great mother. She was so protective when it came to her children, like a mother grizzly. Her mother, Martha, was full of love and a model of modesty. I had the privilege of working with Martha and she made my job as a waiter so easy. She was a good cook and had no inflated ego as many cooks do. My cousin Betty was very loyal to my mother, her aunt. Her offering of support throughout my mother's battle with cancer forever endeared me to her. My family was pretty much all of this and more. We were a simple people, proud of our heritage, but kind and gentle, not demanding center stage. I guess my family's main goal was happiness. It seemed we always took the long way home to get there.

Discrimination and racism were taken for granted at my house, the norm in the life of the LaFountian clan and now by proxy through marriage, the Garlicks. My mother would tell us stories of the LaFountains, discrimination, and ignorance, as if to prepare us for what she anticipated we would eventually encounter growing up. Sadly, her wisdom proved prophetic.

When my sister Patty graduated from eighth grade, Mom wanted to do something special for her, a mother-daughter night. They both dressed up to "beat the band," as Mom described it, and they walked to have dinner at the Yogo Inn, at that time the fanciest restaurant in town. They arrived at the connected hotel and walked into the restaurant. My mother requested a table for two and the manager looked my mother in the eye and told her that would not be possible, as they were booked for the entire night and pretty much the week. Mom looked around and saw many available tables and commented on her observation. The manager replied that those tables were reserved for a later time period. There were no reserved signs on any of the tables. At this point, my mother started getting redder than her "red skin" tone and started seeing red. She knew what was happening, as it would have been very obvious even to the most unaware. As I have mentioned previously, my mother was strikingly beautiful, quite the looker. That night her perfect white teeth were framed by a blazing red lipstick. She often wore high heels and a dress that accented her natural beauty. Unfortunately for this night of celebration

MY EARLY YEARS

she definitely looked like a Native American—beautiful, but nonetheless still Indian.

Mom held it together for the sake of Patty, thanked the manager, and said they would be back in the future when it wasn't so busy. My mother and Patty left and had their mother-daughter celebration elsewhere. When they arrived home it was nearing bed time, so Patty went to bed and Mom told Dad what had happened. Dad tried to comfort Mom and told her to forget about it, as the guy was a jerk and not worth getting upset over. They went to bed, with Mom's blood pressure still high. My mother, not able to sleep, tossed and turned, unable to get the incident out of her head. At 3:00 a.m. Mom got out of bed, went to the phone, and dialed my dad's boss of the lumber yard, who was also a board member for the Yogo Inn. She explained the situation and how she interpreted the meaning—and Al, Dad's boss, also saw it that way. The Yogo's board was called to a meeting the next day; the manager was fired and returned to his home town of New York. Mom never again stepped into the Yogo Inn until I was hired as a busboy at the age of fourteen. I learned from that story what "discrimination" and "racism" looked like and felt like, through the eyes and heart of my mother.

I was the recipient of such ugliness around the age of seven. I was walking home from school one afternoon when a pickup came screeching around the corner. There were two males in the truck. The male in the passenger's side stuck his body out and asked in a shouting voice if my half-breed mother was "on the war path." I could hear them laughing as the truck fishtailed, spitting gravel on my torso and face. I never told Mom what had happened, as I did not want to upset her yet again. Even in the future, when Mom was buying homeowner's insurance from one of the men in the pickup truck, I made the decision to be silent. I am sure he thought I did not recognize him, but his face was branded in my mind; his hypocrisy was a learning tool for how the white human nature worked—at least in Lewistown, Montana. Tear her down, terrorize her son, and take her money. Just who was waging war here?

SEEING THROUGH THE GLASS DARKLY

Cloud of Change...

During my early years of living in Lewistown, I always felt it was a good life. My parents were healthy; they provided for and supported us in our ambitions and goals. We lacked for no essentials, and love was abundant. Things were good for the most part; the hate and scorn for our family did not consume us and we lived with it, never letting its ugliness touch us. But that was about to change, as an invisible, vicious cold front was looming, like an impulsive bully pounding fist into palm. Like a tornado, it would pick up our household and keep spinning until my family was not recognizable, shaking us to our foundations and cracking our core. Perhaps if we'd had a warning, we could have prevented it? Perhaps we were after all just pathetic Indians who could not help but fail, as if it were the prevailing tendency of our spirit, our genes. The first raindrop fell with an enormous thud.

My distant cousin, Monroe, who was at our house quite a bit, reminded me of a James Dean type of character—very cool, good-looking, cocksure. He would always ride his bike over to our house, never coming inside our yard, visiting with me and my sister through the fence that surrounded our house, keeping his distance on the cool side of the fence. I knew that Monroe did not have too much adult supervision, as I picked this up in conversations Mom had about him with other adults in our family. I always enjoyed it when Monroe would come over, always unannounced. I would look up and he would just be there, like the Gods of Cool silently dropped him against the fence, which separated people like Monroe from people like us—"Montana Fonzie."

It had been about a week since we had last seen Monroe, when Mom approached Mary and me in the yard. Monroe, she explained, was hitchhiking and had been killed by the person who had picked him up. I remember being speechless—my mind was having trouble comprehending. Why would anyone want to hurt Monroe? It made no sense to me. He was so cool, handsome...why? Mom proceeded

MY EARLY YEARS

to warn us about hitchhiking, never to do it. There was evil out there, she cautioned, and we had to know its face and understand so that we would be able to stand up to it—or better yet, avoid coming into contact with it. It was my first funeral. I remember watching Monroe's mother at the cemetery, so sad, defeated, I never saw her speak. Later that night the adults went to The Tavern to continue their mourning over alcohol. This would become a family custom, little did I know. Monroe was gone as fast as he would appear before Mary and me. This was the first of many sudden storms. Again, our family in reckless disregard for our safety and well-being, would certainly take the long way home in our search for happiness. Monroe had been looking for a ride, searching for a place to be. He was fifteen.

CHAPTER 3

The Changing Wind

THE COLD FRONT took hold and soon would have her boot heel on our necks, proclaiming that she was well in the lead, having lapped us time and again. I was in the second grade and I could feel another monstrous wind swirling. Patty had been going out with a boy named George, who became a fixture around our family. Patty was crazy about him, and vice versa. George treated our family with much respect, and our parents liked him very much. George would play around with Mary and me, like a loving older brother, the bigger brother I had never experienced. He was often at the supper table, and our parents befriended George's parents, who would visit our home, too. Young love and new connections.

One evening I could hear thunder rumbling in a conversation between my parents, then lightning struck as I learned that George's mother had found out that my mother was a LaFountain. I overheard that George's mother was crying and shocked that her son had actually gone out with a girl who was related to the LaFountains. George's father didn't seem to care, although George's mother would hand down the verdict. She forbade George from dating Patty any longer. George came over that evening, through tears he told my mother what had transpired and what his mother was demanding him to do. George informed my mother that he still wanted to date Patty and he would, despite what his mother's wishes were. My mother told

THE CHANGING WIND

George that even though she disagreed with his mother, he should obey his parents and perhaps in the future they could once again see each other. Both Patty and George were around fifteen, perhaps sixteen when this happened. At the time I did not know what stereotyping was. Years later, George's mother would try to make nice with me when I had to wait on her as a server at the local café. I would have none of it and would remember the hurt and devastation she caused my family because she thought she was better than us.

What followed after the split with George was hurtful and damaging for my sister Patty. Her grades started to suffer; she started to travel with a troubled group of kids; eventually she began to have trouble with the law. Mom and Dad tried desperately to steer Patty back onto the road she was walking before the breakup with George. Anger and distrust seeped into Patty's life, torn from her first love on account of being a LaFountain. She was angry and hurt and a storm was soon raging inside her. Nobody could have predicted how that tempest would be unleashed.

Soon after, Mom and Dad decided to rent our house, which was paid for, and buy the house next door. Why they decided this, I do not know. Both houses were approximately the same size, but the house next door definitely had more curb appeal. We moved into the house that summer and it was a step up. Mom and Dad, during the course of their marriage, had purchased nineteen houses to flip. They made a nice profit on all, which helped to keep our family going all those years. They readied our old house for rental and within a month had it rented.

Central Montana was an area chosen by the US government for underground missile storage. We were still in the Cold War with the Soviet Union, so every few years Lewistown would have an influx of missile workers, and housing would be at a premium. My parents were very fair with the price they charged, $600/month, at one point having been told they could get $1200/month if they so desired. They were satisfied and did not want to be greedy, so they just kept it at $600. They were fortunate the majority of the time, as they were almost constantly able to rent it to missile workers. One such family was black, and our families quickly became friends. They had three sons, roughly the same ages as Mary and me, and we were happy to have them as our friends. Then there was the rest of Lewistown, it seemed.

The mother could not go outside to shake the rugs out without being called "nigger" or "black whore." They were told to go back to Africa and the monkeys where they came from. In school, their boys were treated much the same. Mary and I would come to their defense. We knew discrimination by now and we knew of the hurt and devastation. It put my sister and me at odds with the other students, but we did not care. We, too, were targeted with name-calling. It was actually exhilarating defending someone else for once instead of our own. Their family rented approximately one year from us before they were deployed elsewhere. We had them over for one last meal the night before they would be moving. I remember the mother breaking down, crying, and thanking us for being so good to her family; the father shaking my father's hand, thanking him. My mom told them there was no need to thank us, as we were friends and it was the right and human thing to do. The people of Lewistown were wrong and it was their loss. I was a lucky son to have such parents, people who were able to see the future and knew that peace began in your own back yard. Years earlier, Mom and Dad had been watching Martin Luther King on television, giving his famous "I Have a Dream" speech. Mom was mesmerized. This night before our friends left us, I started to understand what King was saying, and as Mom was enthralled with King, I was spellbound by my parents' actions. I was so proud.

The only other renters that had any importance in my life were a mother and her two sons. The mother was a musician and played regularly in local bars. One son was in high school and the other, Doug, was in my sixth-grade class. It quickly became apparent that the mother had a drinking problem, the older brother had a drug problem, and I had a crush on Doug. I believe both brothers would come over so frequently because Mom was always home and she was easy to talk to. In contrast, their mother was either in the bar playing music, asleep, or getting drunk. My mom, for a short period of time in their lives, acted as a surrogate mother to them.

Doug was handsome, intelligent, witty, and funny. The best thing was he seemed to enjoy my friendship also, at least in the beginning. I would always try to get Doug to come over to our house. I would make up any excuse just to get him over. I invited him to watch TV, have supper, study, play, anything. Doug was also pretty reserved, and I felt miserable when he would decline an invite and exhilarated when he accepted. I pushed hard and I believe that made Doug uncomfortable, as he started distancing himself from me, but not from Mom. He would keep himself at arm's length throughout our junior high years, although he would be pleasant to me, never mean or rude. He and his family moved out of town shortly after eighth grade ended and I never saw or heard from him again. I believe he knew what was going on, he was obviously more mature about sex and feelings than I was, and was not about to go there with me. I, by contrast, had no idea what was happening. I just knew that I really liked Doug and felt good when he was around. I still had my innocence, even though I was starting to have feelings about boys.

In retrospect, I think that everyone knew that I was gay except me. Many people would surmise that I was ignorant, did not want to know the truth, or was scared about the truth and playing dumb. I reject each of these hypotheses. I was a kid and was just being what I thought was natural. No self-judgment or self-doubt. I knew that those would be non-productive and hurtful. Others would pick up the slack for me. I wish I could have stood true to these words.

CHAPTER 4

A Kid Becoming a Man

I WAS THIRTEEN when Charlee, my niece, was born. Patty had one quarter of high school left when she had a run-in with her history teacher. Neither she nor the teacher would budge on the issue, so instead of apologizing to the teacher, Patty just quit school. Within a year she was pregnant. Patty's pregnancy caused my parents so much anxiety and concern. Charlee's father was an obnoxious alcoholic smartass, and would consistently prove that he was incapable of being any type of father to Charlee—even a bad one. He was absent from Charlee's life pretty much until he passed away. Although that might have been a blessing, I hated him for what he did to my sister and also to Charlee. I had fantasies of shooting him dead. Charlee's paternal grandma had nothing to do with Charlee and was despised by my mother; she referred to her as the town whore. I was in the same grade with this woman's daughter, Linda, and sadly I took it out on her, holding her accountable for her brother's actions. We were friends before that, but Patty's pregnancy changed everything. I also lost my friendship with Sally, Linda's best friend, who ultimately had to take sides due to my judging of Linda. Both Linda and Sally tried to reason with me, but anger won out. My own storm raged, and I was a hypocrite, no better than George's mother. I judged Linda because she was the sister of this despicable man; shame on me.

Mom and Dad rented a house for Patty on the other side of town.

They made sure it was furnished and cute for the arrival of the baby. They even tried reaching out to Charlee's father, trying to make the situation bearable. They decided that this was the father of their granddaughter and they should make the best of the situation. Mom invited him over one evening and made hot chocolate. Mom would eventually learn that he was making fun of her and her hot chocolate, saying "how pathetic it was that she did not have something 'stronger' to offer." My parents decided that Patty would be better off without him. Like a drunk falling off his barstool, their fantasy of Charlee growing up with a father collapsed to the floor.

That left me to be the surrogate father to Charlee. Even though I was only thirteen at the time, I was sent to Patty's house at night to watch and care for Charlee, as Mom did not trust Patty's maternal instinct. Mom's intuition was right. Patty would have people over playing poker, drinking, playing loud music. I would go to bed with Charlee right next to me, trying to shield her from the drunken noise—from Patty, her mother, my sister. One early morning as the party mellowed for a moment, Patty came into the bedroom and started slapping Charlee on the face until she started to cry. I tried to shield Charlee from the slapping only to have Patty's abuse focus on me. I remember crying and feeling humiliated. Patty seemed oddly energized by this—taunting me, calling me a baby, and asking what I was going to do about it. She finally tired of slapping me and sat on the end of the bed. She kept looking at Charlee and finally spoke these words to her: "I try to hate you because of him, but I just can't." She then got up and went into the living room, where she passed out on the couch.

Listening for a clue that would tell me she indeed had passed out, I heard the beautiful silence. I very carefully and slowly got up from the bed and went out into the living room where I saw Patty sleeping. I would go back into the bedroom where I would pull Charlee close to me and fall asleep crying, a kid protecting a baby. I indeed was not a young man; a man would not have cried, I told myself. A man would have defended himself. My heart started to harden against alcoholics.

SEEING THROUGH THE GLASS DARKLY

They did not have a disease; they were just very skilled, self-centered manipulators. Their thoughts were only of "me, me, me," and when they were done with thoughts of "me" they would start to think of "me, me, and me" once more.

Over the next few years, I was introduced to Al-Anon, to those who were trying to find understanding and support for themselves in trying to deal with their loved one's alcohol problems. I did not have a choice in deciding whether or not I attended these meetings; it was decided for me by my mother. She thought it would help the family in coping with this horrible "disease" and ultimately help Patty. I hated the whole process and my tolerance of these people grew even thinner. I wanted to say "Screw you, Bill W.; you are no friend of mine."

Around the same time, Leland went on a drinking binge one weekend. This behavior was not typical of Leland. He was a hard-working man, responsible, and loving to his family. He would drink a beer or two, but never to my knowledge to the point where his reasoning went out the window. My parents received a phone call telling them that Leland was holding a gun to his head and was threatening to kill himself. I was immediately sent over to Leland's home, just two blocks away. Send the kid. I have no idea why I was sent over, given that we were not that close, and I certainly did not know what to say or do to convince my brother that blowing his head off would be a very bad idea for all concerned. I walked into the front room of their mobile home and saw Leland sitting on a stool holding the gun to his head, talking in a slow slur. He was babbling that he should just end his life, no one cared, and we were all assholes. With him were his wife, and Marvin and his wife. They were all trying to talk him into putting the gun down, asking him why he would want to do such a thing, telling him things were not that bad and certainly would get better if he would just wait for tomorrow's arrival he would see they were right.

I sat in silence, just listening, watching, feeling betrayed by him. This continued for well over an hour. I grew agitated. It was a beautiful day out, I had no homework, Mom did not need any help with

Billy, there were no babies to watch, I could be enjoying the day—but here I was, with another of Bill's friends. My thoughts began to fester in my mind, my blood pressure slowly rising, my heart quickening. I began to shake. I was oddly enraged. I then talked myself down from this ledge I was building in my mind: not a ledge for myself, but a ledge for Leland. God, I wanted to push him off, into what or where I didn't know, and frankly didn't care, but anything would be better than this. I closed my eyes and went through many cycles of this scenario and my anger. Then when I could not take it any longer, I got up and shouted at Leland, "For Christ's sake if you're going to shoot your fucking head off, do it—I am tired of this. I could be enjoying the day, but I have to waste it because of you."

Marvin shouted at me, "Johnny, no!"

I quickly gained my composure and I calmly told Leland, "Just do it—stop holding us hostage."

Leland was silent, then started to laugh. "At last, someone who has some balls to tell me off" was his response. I looked at him and shook my head as I headed out the door. The rest of the day I do not remember.

I have always thought of Mom when remembering this story. She had experienced a similar incident with her father, who came home drunk one night, with rifle in hand, threatening yet again to kill the entire family before a new sun would rise. This particular night, my grandfather was especially worked up and was meaner than usual. In the course of threatening the family, he slapped my grandmother very hard across her face, breaking her lip open. My mother, with years of anger bottled up inside of her, could take no more. She jumped across the room and slapped her father across the face as hard as she could, in the process hurting her hand. She screamed at him, telling him that her mom did not deserve this treatment from him and to never hit her again, otherwise she would be using that loaded gun on him. My mother recounted to me that she fell silent, trembling with fear, and horrible thoughts in her mind of what might transpire in the next few seconds. My grandfather said nothing, put the rifle down, and left the house. He never touched another drink for the remainder of his life. My mom said if she had known it would be that easy to get him to stop drinking, she would have slapped him silly years earlier.

Life during this period of my life was a mixture of tests, struggles, and just getting by. I did not need the name Coyote after all; my family was giving me all the character I needed. Patty got pregnant with another niece for me, JoJo, by another man who would prove to be no father to JoJo. Like Charlee's father, he was not even a bad father, which would imply being present. Deadbeat 2.0. I was getting proficient at changing a diaper, rocking my nieces to sleep, and feeding and burping. I very well may have had more responsibilities than facial hairs. Dad was still working six days a week and we were still dirt poor. Billy was slowly going downhill, his latest stroke leaving him completely paralyzed and unable to feed himself. I would help him with his feeding—mainly baby food. There were some jars he did not like and it was a battle getting him to eat certain ones. I would help him out of this dilemma when Mom or Dad was not looking, I would eat it for him. I actually grew to like the taste of certain baby foods. I was killing two birds with one stone. There was no objection from Billy, and we grew closer.

At this early time in my life I became more and more interested in music. I had already been learning the accordion and was taking organ lessons from Mrs. Story. She was a dear soul and taught me the basics. Previously during the sixth grade I formed a band called The Vagabonds, consisting of me on the accordion, Mary on the organ, and Natalie, a friend from fifth grade through high school, on the drums. We had a great time for one summer and entered the local parade, where we won first place. Later in high school, Natalie and I would again form a band. We played at some dances and actually got paid doing what we loved. Natalie killed Carole King's "It's Too Late." One of my few genuine friends, she actually made my life easier, especially in high school, and was my saving grace many times.

Knowing that Mrs. Story was probably not the best music teacher, Mom devised a plan; she would take me to see this lady who was in a wheelchair, a gifted piano teacher, Louise McLaughlin. Mom told her I was gifted and if she would take me on as a student, she would not regret it. There was one catch; we did not have the money to pay. Mom told Louise that my dad and I would paint her house from top to bottom; she would have to supply the paint. I would also do errands for Louise as additional payment in exchange for the lessons. By this time, Louise was literally rolling her eyes. How many times had she heard how "gifted" one's child was? Mom was relentless, and she would not take no for an answer.

What resulted was a dear relationship with a woman who had overcome polio and who became self-reliant. Louise also introduced me to the Mormon religion. I did not embrace her religion, but it gave me an understanding of their faith. I would often play piano for their services on Sunday mornings; it was an eye-opener and widened my views on the world. It would prove to be valuable years later when I was searching different religions and spirituality. Louise told my parents years later that she was very blessed when we walked into her home, although I believe we were the blessed. I was introduced to Louise's family and I was there when Louise's brother passed away. Louise was there for me when my brother Billy and both my parents died. I watched Louise grow old and I visited her regularly for several years in the nursing home before her passing. She gave me the gift of music.

Then there was junior high school. If this was a prelude to high school and what I might expect from the future, things were not looking good for me. My saving grace was again music. My band teacher was Mr. Irons, a nice-looking man in his 40s—slender, black hair, glasses. His love for music was contagious. He began teaching me the clarinet while I was in the fifth grade. He was a gentle man, intelligent, and had a gift of being able to explain music concepts in a way that I could easily understand. He introduced me to Latin and the meanings of the words that would translate so beautifully for my music understanding. Mr. Irons took a liking to all of his students and gave 120% of himself. One summer between sixth and seventh grade

SEEING THROUGH THE GLASS DARKLY

Mr. Irons paid me a visit at our home to see how I was doing. He asked if I was having any problems or had any questions about music that he could help me with, showing how truly dedicated he was to his students.

At this time in my life, I started remembering incidents by attaching them to songs that were popular during that period. Mr. Irons was "Bridge over Troubled Water" by Simon and Garfunkel. I remember coming to band practice at 7:00 a.m. after getting up at 5:00 a.m. and practicing piano for an hour before heading out to school, and hearing that song in the hallways as I approached the band room. Mr. Irons kept playing that song over and over; he was mesmerized by it and repeatedly played it, much like a teenager would to drive one's parents crazy. Mr. Irons was young at heart, and it was easy to see and easy to like him for it. We had band practice three times a week and those mornings tended to lead to better days.

We had a rotating schedule that changed every day, so except for band practice, which was extracurricular, we would go through a whole rotation every seven days. During the class before Physical Education (PE), I would start to physically feel ill. I knew that bullying, hitting, and sexual abuse were on the class syllabus every day. I tried to stay away from the jocks and the popular guys, as hopefully they would not notice me and I would be under their radar for the guy to be picked upon for that day. Usually this would not work; I was pretty much the flavor of the day and would get shoved to the ground, elbowed in the face, or worse—slammed against the lockers after getting out of the shower still naked. After I was pushed to the lockers the popular jocks would pretend they were fucking me while telling me how I was enjoying it; all the while, I was crying. It was always the macho types that took this role of pretending to screw me, calling me a queer, faggot, homo, any hurtful name depicting the disgusting gay boy, after they were done doing their motions.

Teachers never seemed to be around while these incidents were happening. I was too busy trying to protect my face or get my clothes back on as fast as I possibly could and get out of there to wonder where the adults were. I would go to the next class and slowly regain my composure, stop the trembling, hide the shame, and calm my racing heart. For the next six years, I would cry while walking to school, desperately wanting it to be over—I hated it. Many times I thought of suicide, I was so lonely and miserable. My Catholic upbringing saved me; guilt prevented me from committing the one sin that would be unforgivable: suicide. For nine months of the year, I would go through the emotions of going to school, talk myself out of doing the unforgivable, read *Dear Abby* and take her advice to wait twenty-four hours. Painful, but it worked.

In hindsight, these were most certainly "straight as an arrow" boys assaulting me and pretending to engage in sexual intercourse with me, engaging in what psychoanalytic theory refers to as "reaction formation"—a defense used to manage anxiety stemming from the presence of unacceptable feelings and impulses. There is the porn addict who sacrifices his life attending anti-porn rallies and lobbying for legislative bans on pornography; there is the man who strongly dislikes a woman treating her in an excessively kind and even flirtatious manner; and there are Central Montana jocks made intolerably anxious by budding sexual feelings for other boys engaging in bullying, harassment, and perhaps even getting sexual gratification from the "pretend" act of having anal sex with a "despised" peer. For you *Glee* fans, I wonder how many Dave Karofskys were in that locker room, dealing with their gay impulses by bullying and assaulting me, alias: "Spud," their special version of Kurt Hummel.

The autumn of seventh grade, I started washing dishes at the Fergus Café. Being underage, I was paid under the table and received free meals. I would work after school and on the weekends, many times the graveyard shift, when all the drunks would converge after the bars closed. Working took me away from child-rearing and took my mind off of the torment that was school. I was a hard worker, always on time, polite, conscientious, and tried to do more than my employer expected of me. My family needed the money badly and I was not about to mess up any opportunity that came my way. This good work ethic paid off and soon I was waiting on tables—mainly the graveyard shift on the weekends —but now, in addition to getting an hourly wage of $2.50, I was also receiving tips. This helped out my family greatly and I felt like I was contributing and doing my fair share. This early experience prepared me in obtaining and always having a job when others were unemployed. I was good with people, had good communication skills, and most important, I always tried to please the people I was working around, be it co-workers, customers, or supervisors.

I always remembered my parents telling me that having a job meant that I had a contract with my employer. That contract included a rate of pay that both parties had agreed upon, a time frame when I would be available for my employer, and an unwritten stipulation never to be too proud to do anything that my employer asked of me, as long as it was ethical. Whenever I hear of people complaining about their jobs (i.e., too little pay, too much work, "I don't get paid to do that") I always think back to my parents' advice. It has paid off for me and has worked for me my entire life.

So with work, school, watching kids, music, gardening, and Al-Anon, there was really not much time for anything else in my life. I was busy, unhappy, and worried. What might possibly happen at school was always at the forefront of my thoughts—gym, showers, and lockers. I never shared this with anyone, ashamed that I might be the reason for all of the abuse and bullying being perpetrated on me. If my family found out, I would be devastated. I was not gay, I was not weak, and I did not need Al-Anon. I was just a caring person in a family of Landless Indians that was going through rough times. I did benefit from taking things "one day at a time," as I was trying to survive psychologically, hold back the tears, and not become so fearful of the bullying that I would kill myself. Like *Dear Abby* hinted: "It will get better...."

CHAPTER 5

It Will Get Better

IT WILL GET better, it will get better, it will get better; that became my mantra. I would say this over and over in my mind as if these words would conjure up a magic spell and the transformation in my life would be astonishing. Perhaps it did work a little spell on my freshman year of high school.

At this time in my family's life, Father Boyer of the Episcopalian Church came into our lives, a major player in Patty's life in her "redemption"—more practical than spiritual—and a major admirer of Mom for her principled behavior and moral compass. Father Boyer's influence in my life was fleeting, but he showed me another world of powerful possibilities that would give me a chance at making a real escape from Lewistown. Father Boyer had a soft spot for the Native American. I guess maybe that was one of the reasons he and his wife responded well to our family. Just before the spring preceding my freshman year of high school, Father Boyer came to our house with some news he thought we would like to hear. There was a program for Native American teenagers entering high school, much like a foreign exchange program. Father Boyer wanted me to take a number of tests and, if I scored high enough, I would be accepted. This would mean that I would be spending not just my freshman year, but all four years of high school, abroad. I was to choose three different areas in the world, the United States included. Father Boyer asked my parents if they would be willing to let me do this, and my parents said yes. He had brought the papers with him, so I filled the papers out that afternoon and chose my fantasy high school placements. My first choice was Switzerland, second was Italy, and third was Hawaii. I was to travel with Father Boyer that next week to the reservation where the tests were being given. My fantasies engulfed me, imagining life beyond the confinements and prejudice of Lewistown. Europe? Hawaii? Was this God? Fate? Whatever it was, I felt an eager hopefulness. To my bullies it was, "Screw you, I have a flight to catch."

The next week, Father Boyer and I made the two hour trip to the Rocky Boy Indian Reservation. Filled with trepidation that I would fail, I entered the room where the test was being administered. There were about ten other Indian teenagers, obviously full-blooded. I must have looked like a senator's son to this crowd. The testing took around two hours to complete. Father Boyer, anxiously waiting outside in the hallway, asked me how I thought I had done when I exited the room. I thought I had done well and I felt confident that I had passed and would soon be packing my suitcases, which reminded me that we did not own any suitcases. The results would be one month off and the wait was going to be brutal. My life was hanging in the balance, it seemed.

Sadly, Dad had his heart attack that April, right before Easter. My family needed me now more than ever, especially my mother. I never asked about my test results. My fantasy was over, and I did not want passing test scores to fuel resentment and a sense of loss. I was a mama's boy, and there really was no deliberation about what to do.

So with much disappointment and fear, I entered high school—no suitcases, but plenty of baggage. I really did not know what to expect. My freshman class numbered around 170. Since high school was bigger, perhaps I could just find a way to be lost in the crowd. Perhaps I would just get more bullying, because there were more bullies. I got my class schedule and fumbled around the halls trying to find the classrooms and trying not to be tardy. Around sixth period, on my first day, I entered the study hall, which was connected to the library. It was a big room that sat roughly 150-200 students. Each student was assigned a specific seat for the quarter. I landed between two seniors: a doctor's son behind me, and his best friend directly in front of me. It was rumored that this doctor's son was quite different—"sleeps in a coffin" different. I thought he was cool and confident, and figured out quickly that his friend was along for the ride. I found these two guys to be great, my study hall friends for the year. They seemed to like me, they did not torment me, and we had a solid but superficial connection. We were not best buddies, but for me it was a respite from the daily torment that I came to expect as the norm in my life. So, I actually looked forward to going to study hall each 6th period.

In comparison to my last three years in high school, my freshman year was the least horrible. My sister Mary was a junior, and we were in the same building again, but this time she seemed to want to keep her distance from me. I believe she did not want to be associated with her brother, the queer. I had managed to survive on my own and I was pretty much a loner anyway, so it really did not matter.

Mary had started experimenting with drugs and alcohol by this time, and the police were beginning to know Mary on a first-name basis. Patty was having her own troubles with the law, perhaps due to the burden of being a single parent to two daughters. Her brushes with the law cost her jail time and a soiled reputation in Lewistown. Mom blamed Mary's behavior in part on Patty. She felt that Mary had always admired Patty and perhaps was trying to emulate her sister by following her down the road that would cause only grief for her and her family. I believe Mary had her own mind and chose the path she was going down. I remember many times coming home and Mary had run away, gotten high, or was expelled from school. The list went on.

Yet Mary miraculously held on to her job working in a small local meat cutting plant. The owner loved Mary and her work and was always stopping by the house to tell my parents what a good job she was doing. How she kept this job while using drugs and alcohol, and periodically disappearing, I will never understand. Patty managed to

◄ SEEING THROUGH THE GLASS DARKLY

get her GED, and through AA and friends was becoming more and more involved with the probation office, both as a probationer and as a clerical worker. Patty was showing an interest in the law enforcement field, specifically the probation department. She was coming full circle.

Upon entering high school, I was thirteen years old. This had happened because I was four when I started kindergarten. They had not yet passed the law that a child had to be the minimum age of five when entering kindergarten, so I had a head start. That September after I turned fourteen, Mom contacted Marie, the woman in charge of hiring at Yogo Inn. Mom personally knew Marie, so she thought this might increase my chances of being hired. Marie came to our house to interview me for the position of busboy. She was around sixty, proper in her speech, dress, and demeanor. After about fifteen minutes of asking questions, she left and told us that she would be in touch. True to her word, she came back to our house two days later. She said she was impressed with my answers and doubly impressed with my eagerness to want to work. She had one worry: my age. She said to legally hire me I would have to be fifteen and she did not know if she would be able to get the paperwork through. We would have to do some manipulation with the truth—a little white lie. My mother took over the conversation and assured Marie that if she would just hire me, she would not regret her decision, and any papers that I would need to sign I would sign, no questions. Mom asked her to just give me a chance. Marie sat quietly in the chair for about thirty seconds, looked up, and said, "Okay, John, you are hired." I started work two days later.

Working at Yogo Inn came to be a major part of my high school years. I started working two or three evenings a week, then soon it was three or four evenings. Within six months I was working close to forty hours a week. Friday nights, especially if there was a convention in town, I might work eight hours, sometimes till midnight or 1:00 a.m. Saturdays and Sundays it was guaranteed that I would work a minimum of eight hours per day, sometimes double-shifting. Getting all those hours on the weekend meant I could work less on the weekdays and still keep up my school work. I made the honor roll every quarter of every year in high school, graduating at the top ten percent as the youngest person in my class. Soon I was promoted to head of the busboys and writing the schedule. When I turned fifteen, I was given the opportunity to bus in the bar, which I gladly accepted. Yogo's bar was the fanciest in town, where all the higher-class people came to drink and dine. I liked the clientele and I was very at ease with this type of work. Soon I was given the opportunity to serve drinks, even though I was not yet eighteen. Lewistown being the small community it was, a blind eye was turned. Although I had an aversion to drinking and drunks, Yogo's bar was not the scuzzy type of bar that I had become accustomed to because of my family's problems. I accepted and soon learned all of the abbreviations and language to serve booze with efficiency. The tips were great, and I was making more money than I had ever had in my life.

The next opportunity that Yogo gave me was to be a "Chippendales" server, along with three other guys. This was Lewistown's version of the "girls' night out" colliding with the "boy next door" image. I was perfect for the part. My physique was that of a swimmer—lean, muscular, and young. With our black pants, bare smooth chests, and bow ties, the "Chippendales" Wednesday night was a success.

After that stint, I was offered the position of server, which was the job I had wanted all along. This position would give me the best money and the best hours in conjunction with school. I kept this position until the spring of my senior year, when I quit due to a disagreement with management that could not be worked out. I cannot even recall what the disagreement was about, but I know how stubborn I had become. I am certain that I overreacted. I prefer to call it passion —a quality if harnessed would help me to achieve in all areas, to be a caring provider and lover, but it would be my Achilles' heel many times. I just needed to be careful that my Paris would not shoot his arrow there.

CHAPTER 6

The Wonder Years

I STILL WONDER at times how I made it out of high school alive—literally. My high school years were the worst part, in the most extreme degree, of growing up. The grief given by other students never let up, the hatred shown me never stopped, the bullying was grade AAA. I am only thankful the internet was not around, because the respite between the times I got out of school to when I went back saved me. I would have been a prime target on Facebook and I am certain that cyber-torment would have resulted in my suicide.

The torture began in earnest during my sophomore year, every class. At the beginning of the school year, I started to break out with very bad acne. My whole face was covered with pimples and hard pustules. I would wash my face continually with hot soapy water and put alcohol on my face, trying to dry them up. I would squeeze them and make them pop, trying to get the "poison" out of my face. The squeezing just scarred my face and it made for a very vicious cycle. The popular guys, the jocks, started calling me names. Crater Face, Zit Face, Gravel Face were some of the more popular, but the one that was most popular was "Spud," the rough, pitted surface of a potato that would go from the sack to the trash. The kids seemed to forget my real name and "Spud" became my name for the next three years.

Music was my saving grace once again in my life and, of the friends I did have, most were either in the band or choir. Our choir group, called A Cappella, was amazing and beautiful to me. I began to provide the piano accompaniment. There was a girl who was a better pianist, but she was not able to do all the accompanying—so have a seat, Spud, you're the next-best piano player. The director of A Cappella was strict, and if you messed up once accompanying his choir, no problem, everyone makes mistakes; mess up twice, God help you. That is why I really did not want to accompany for him. He took all the fun and beauty out of it for me and gave me yet another thing to worry about. I did do a lot of accompaniment for students entering vocal competitions locally and statewide, so it did make me "popular" in that circle. Natalie was one friend I loved to accompany. She would work with me and tell me what she wanted from me; in turn, I would try to do my best for her because I wanted her to shine as brightly as possible. Dave was also another friend, who was pretty much the same caliber as Natalie. He was an outstanding singer and was very popular in school. I almost felt cool. Besides band and choir, I was also in a six-member rock/pop band. I found some acceptance with this band, and we had a blast, playing for groups, dances, events. One gig we had consistently was playing for dances at the local country club every Friday/Saturday night. The group was even contacted once by a record company for a possible signing. We never made the cut, but the guy provided us with good critiques and suggestions and it certainly was far better than anything we had ever imagined would happen to us.

But besides my music, I was in a private hell. I had no sanctuary I could escape to while in school and my stomach was in a perpetual knot, great for my six-pack abs but rough on my digestion and nerves. No matter what class I was in, there was a jock scorning me. Spud was an easy target. I drew inward, scared and hating my life. I got it drilled into my head that I was physically ugly, disgusting to be viewed. Spud the Elephant Man. I felt like Joseph Merrick, and grew to have a soft spot in my heart for our lot. I admired Joseph's tact and intelligence, and mostly his kindness toward others when he himself was in such agony. I hoped after this hell ended that some kindness might still be left inside me for others. I feared that I would live a life of bitterness and resentment. I could have been in Honolulu or Zurich. I just wanted a chance to have a small portion of the character of Joseph.

Although I was quite fit and agile, I hated sports. Every year in PE, the class had to do a full week of playing a different sport. Let's talk about basketball. In short, kids do not steal the ball from a popular jock. Contrary to Spud's role at school, I made that mistake by sneaking up behind a strapping young fellow, and proceeded to take the ball and dribble it toward our basket. I passed the ball to someone more adept at shooting. We scored. Then the prison rules kicked in. All of the jocks got together, even the ones on my team, and surrounded me, forcing me into a corner of the gymnasium. I heard the offended jock's voice telling me to look up. I said no. We went back and forth with this, my eyes planted on a spot on the floor.

The mob raged. Some of the other jocks grabbed my face and maneuvered me in position so I was now facing the one from whom I stole the ball. He had the basketball in his hands and repeatedly pounded it against my face. I grew bloody. My nose was likely broken. They told me to think the next time before I did something stupid like that again. Basketball lesson learned. I have no idea where our teacher was. Perhaps he might have been thinking of ways to incorporate good sportsmanship into the lesson, but never got around to sharing his thoughts. Perhaps he did not give a shit. Not once did the adults of Fergus County High School intervene while I was being physically injured or verbally abused. Maybe they called me "Spud" in the teachers' lounge—the gay kid with acne. The lack of intervention or even consolation made them accessories.

Showering after PE was mandatory. I would always try to be the first one in before the other guys got there so I could get out and be dressed before they arrived to take their showers. One Friday our teacher was absent. His substitute, it turns out, was absent too, in the supervising department. I had gotten in and taken my shower, got dressed, and thought I was in the clear. I had no idea the jocks had a special event planned for me that day. They came toward me, surrounded me, and then held me down; they took all my clothes off, hitting me, while I was trying to defend myself. Then four guys proceeded to carry me, with two guys holding one arm each and two guys holding one leg each. They carried me around, with everyone else in the class right behind them—even those who were also picked on by these jocks. I was on parade. I heard laughing and boisterous yelling. I was screaming and crying, begging them please to let me go. I would not tell anyone, just let me go. They carried me into the girls' locker room and threw me on the floor, without my clothes. They ran to the boys' locker room and locked the door. A group of girls stood staring at me, their eyes widening, covering their mouths as they started to laugh. Spud had been peeled and dumped onto the floor of the girls' locker room. Again there were no adults around. Humiliated, embarrassed, sickened, I tried to cover myself from the awkwardness of adolescence, ashamed of my body. I don't remember getting back into the locker room. I do not remember getting dressed. I just don't remember anything after that.

Nothing ever came of this incident, or anything else that happened to me while in high school. I did not press for any retribution for any of these incidents, so those in authority have a way out, I guess; I'm sure they would say it was my fault—I should have come forward, but I don't believe that nobody in authority ever saw anything that happened to me. I believe I was not important to them. I was an Indian—but most disgusting, I was a queer.

CHAPTER 7

Winding It Down

MY HIGH SCHOOL years dragged on for me; similar incidents came and went. Remarkably, I was able to gain a certain respect from some of the jocks. Their childish antics were not playful, just tiresome and irksome. One jock's latest prank was waiting for me to come down the hallway and hit my books with his hand as hard as possible so everything I was carrying would scatter. I would try to avoid going down "his" hallway, but to get to certain classrooms I had no choice. After a few months I was so depressed, and tired of collecting my belongings off the hallway floors and sorting papers back to where they belonged. I went through the typical "ledge-building" with this jock as I had done with my brother Leland years before. I would build the ledge I wanted to push this jock off of, and then disassemble it in my mind with the usual racing heart, rising blood pressure, etc. I wanted to punch him in the face before he hit my books. I knew this would bring repercussions, but I was so done, tired, and angry.

The next week, I was going to French class and I saw this jock down the hall. I had to pass him. I braced myself and quickly built his ledge, I held fast and did not tear it down as I neared him. Out of the corner of my eye, I saw his hand aiming for my books; my right fist aimed for his face and I connected. He was shocked—hell, I was shocked. I had put him on his heels and I was not going to wait for a response. I quickened my pace and entered French class as fast as

WINDING IT DOWN

I could.

Retribution came swiftly. The next day around the same time I was at my locker, kneeling on the floor, getting my materials for French class. I heard a voice say "John." I looked up and was met with a fist delivered with an under punch to my nose. My body was thrown back by the force—I landed on my back, blood squirting everywhere; it took my breath away, it hurt so much. This pop star jock told me this was payback. Dazed, I went to French class. Late, I knocked on the door. Henrietta, my teacher, answered, looked at me, and pulled me in asking what had happened. I told her nothing had happened. I did not want a repeat. She helped me clean up, washed my shirt, and gave me a blanket while my shirt dried. The jocks never knocked my books to the floor again; I never punched any of them in the face again.

Junior and senior years came and went, along with the proms and senior breakfast. I did not attend any of these events. I had no one to go with. I had isolated myself even from the band and A Cappella. If I did attend by myself, the odds were that I would be the guy who was the joke of the party. Some students attended "alone." The biggest reason for my not attending was that I felt ugly. It had been drilled into my head the last four years how disgusting I looked. This, along with the fact that it would have been a hardship on my family and me to use money for the price of the breakfast, the tuxes, and whatever else there might be.

I ostracized myself further from my classmates by not attending these social events. Almost all the students would be talking on Monday about what a great time they had had that weekend; it seemed almost like a formal social debut or a cotillion ball, where the young females and males of Lewistown were being introduced into society to take over the reins from their parents. They had the basic skills of spitefulness, pettiness, cruelty, intolerance; they were ready to enter Lewistown's society. My classmates had to learn those traits from someone; I believe that probably would have been their parents. I might be wrong; maybe my classmates were inherently bad people, their elements of meanness and cruelty perhaps existing since their births. Maybe it was just plain simple: they were bullies and their parents had no clue, much like the school authorities. I have spent my entire life trying to make sense of their hatred toward me and have not been able to come up with a reasonable answer. I told my partner Clayton that perhaps in writing this book I might gain some type of closure and perhaps some type of healing. I do not know yet as I write this—all I know is that once again my heart races and negative thoughts return.

Those Silent Heroes:

It would be unfair of me to end this chapter without giving thanks to my classmates who did stand up for me. Those acts of kindness and bravery toward me, I am sure they were unaware of; they probably did not even know I considered them as such. There are always two sides to each story, and for me here is the positive side.

One such act consisted of both kindness and bravery; at least that is how I interpreted this person's actions. I was in stenography class—and yes, you guessed it, I was the only male. One afternoon right before class was to begin and everyone was getting back from lunch, I was in my seat studying my steno notes. There were a few girls, also; the teacher had not yet arrived. Once again one of the popular jocks stuck his head in and asked me why I was taking a class that only girls took. I kept my silence. Gail, a very popular girl, was taking the class and was there studying also. She looked up and told him: "Why don't you leave John alone, he is doing nothing to you. And by the way, you idiot, you have to be smart to take this class." He had nothing to say to Gail and retreated down the hall. I felt a smile coming to my face and thanked Gail. She told me that I did not need to thank her, and she was just tired of this person being a moron.

Another incident involved Natalie. It was graduation day and the ceremonies had just ended; everyone was outside in a celebratory mood. I was with my family and we were about to head home when

Natalie came bouncing over in her usual effervescent mood, congratulating me and telling me that she had to get a picture with me for her yearbook. This was an act so small, yet so big to me. Her kindness filled my heart. I have often thought it was a good thing for her that she was a woman. Had she been a guy and gay I would have gone after her with all my heart. This young woman was pretty, and she always had such a beautiful soul. Natalie, I thank you from the bottom of my heart for being such a good friend to me all those years—again, you will never know…I was a lucky friend.

There were other such acts of kindness sent my way, such people as Kent, Neal, John, Debbie, Janice, Deb, Susan, Kim, Patti, Dennis. The biggest thing they did was that they were all civil to me and did not play cruel tricks on me. For this I am forever grateful and thankful.

CHAPTER 8

Free at Last, Free at Last

HAVING LISTENED TO Martin Luther King Jr.'s speech, "I Have a Dream" many times, I felt I had reached my promised land when I graduated from high school. No more would I have to endure the bullying, violence, hatred, the persecution, and the discrimination of being...of being what? Was it because I had acne vulgaris, because I was an Indian, because people could see the gay tendencies that I did not see? Like a black person who is discriminated against because they have a darker skin tone, the discrimination and cruelty sent my way were just as ignorant, mindless, and idiotic. How it is that one's race or physical features makes one so undesirable that those who put themselves in a seat of judgment must resort to violence and cruelty? Are certain family lines still evolving? Is their mind only an extension of their physical brain, unable to manifest their consciousness and bring them to a higher state of existence, to being civil and tolerant? That complex, which we refer to as our mind, that source of cognitive faculties that enables one's consciousness—thinking, reasoning, perception, and judgment—does it, in those people who carry discrimination to its lowest level, not have the capability for compassion and caring? Perhaps not. Whatever the reason, I feel no hatred toward those people. I feel no love or empathy, either. I just want nothing to do with them; they are negative energy, and gravity is hard enough to fight as one gets older. I do not need anything else that will ultimately drag me down.

FREE AT LAST, FREE AT LAST

The summer following high school graduation was one of relief. No longer would I feel intense fear and anxiety walking to school. No longer would I stumble down the school hallways because I was too embarrassed to raise my face to see where I was going, but instead would trip over something in my path. No longer would I be bullied. No longer would I have to do many things I hated simply because people hated me. It was my summer of freedom and I looked forward to that autumn entering college. I was accepted into Montana State University in Bozeman. I would major in business with a minor in music. My two sisters decided that they would also attend MSU. Our parents helped us move down there, and Patty got family housing, I was in the dorm, and Mary rented a trailer home. Within the month, it was clear that Patty would need help with the two girls, so I moved in with her and in the process saved some money. We had scheduled our classes so either Patty or I would be free to watch the girls, while the other attended class. During the weekend when the weather was still good enough to drive back to Lewistown, I would go back home to work in the Fergus Café and earn a little extra money for school. Between classes, working, watching Charlee and JoJo, my college grades suffered. I just wanted to pass and graduate.

After the first year, Mary dropped out and moved back to Nebraska, where she had already completed a year at a Christian college. After about a year of helping Patty with the kids, she met a guy, Gary, who would be her future husband. I decided to move out and get my own apartment, where I also worked as a maintenance guy around the complex. This eliminated the need to travel to Lewistown for work, which freed up a lot of time for me. That summer Patty and Gary married and had their first child, a son, whom they named Shane. Gary was a ranger at Yellowstone National Park, so his job would take him away Sunday night and he would not return till the following Friday night. So even though Patty was no longer a single parent, she still needed help watching the kids. Luckily I had not forgotten how to change a diaper.

At MSU no one really cared who or what I was. The students

seemed to be more mature in that aspect. I was still a loner and did not have much of a social life. I still felt awkward and ugly around people and was very shy. Not until I reach my second year of college did I start to have any semblance of a social life. I had signed up for sign language the first semester of my second year, and found a new circle of friends instantly. We all had a love for the language and would hang around after classes practicing signing and take our practicing down to Saint George's Dragon Pub. The following semester I signed up for the second course in sign language and had a repeat of my last semester. That summer I signed up to help deaf students who would be coming to Bozeman for a month of camp. It was a summer that was frustrating because the students were much more adapt and faster at signing their own language than I was. The other students in my class struggled, too. But it was also a summer that had its reward at the end of camp. By the time camp drew to a close, we were signing almost as fast as the hearing-impaired campers.

One day, I just started signing and keeping up with them. I watched my fingers in bewilderment, perplexed that they were keeping up with everyone else. Finally after all the practicing and fumbling, the movements were kicking in. I was ecstatic. My last year, I tried out for the Signing Theatre, but did not make it. My friends who had been in it the year before had gotten so good at the art that I, the novice, could not compete with the artistic abilities they had honed the year previous. It was fun while it lasted. That winter I signed up for downhill skiing—I was going to have fun my last winter there. I would go skiing every Friday afternoon and had a blast. Downhill skiing came easy for me and I enjoyed it very much—I received credit toward for my degree, with the added advantage of not being assaulted or stripped naked. What could be finer? Going to summer school and taking no breaks, I completed college in three years.

CHAPTER 9

Back Home

AFTER GRADUATING FROM college in 1978, I headed back to Lewistown. Having no job prospects, not even a job interview lined up, I started wondering if I had wasted the last three years of my life going to college. The answer to that question I believe was ultimately yes. In the future, I would never really use my college diploma, and the jobs I would get would be either by experience or would have nothing to do with the field I graduated in. I got a job waiting tables and lived at home with my parents. By the following spring, I was dissatisfied with myself and my lack of accomplishments; I felt like a failure and needed to do something more meaningful with my life. I needed to get out of Lewistown. I had two friends who were living in Hawaii at the time, and because Hawaii had always been my dream place to visit since I was five, I was invited to visit. I bought a one-way ticket to Hawaii, imagining that I would stay with them until I found a job; then I would get my own place. That idea quickly vanished when the parents of these two girls said it would look improper for a guy to be living with their daughters. Little did they really know. Plan B.

Plan B consisted of Bonita Springs, Florida. In Bonita Springs there was an organic farm and health spa called the Shangri-La. They were looking for people to maintain the grounds and gardens in exchange for room and board. I applied and was accepted. I traded in my ticket to Hawaii for my new destination of Bonita Springs. Bonita

SEEING THROUGH THE GLASS DARKLY

Springs turned out to be a nice place to work and I learned about the natural health practices that were taught there. I stayed in Florida for six months and again wanted something different. I returned home once again, but just to get a change of clothes. The following spring I packed my bags and headed off to Yellowstone National Park to work at Old Faithful Inn Restaurant.

Working at Yellowstone Park was pretty much like the movie *Dirty Dancing*. The workers were young, there was usually a party every night, and there was an excitement for me about just being with others of my own age. My acne had subsided and although I had some scarring, at least I did not have to deal with people calling me Spud or making insensitive remarks about the way I looked. My sister Patty was living in Mammoth at the time with her family, which now included one other nephew, Shawn. She now had four children and her husband Gary. She seemed happy that I was there, and I was happy to be there. To work at Yellowstone you had to meet certain criteria and most establishments were strict in their policies. Great customer service meant plenty of servers. This caused a problem in short order. There were so many servers that it was almost impossible to make more than $50 a night. I had visions of making at least a $100 a night, even thinking it would be possible to hit $150-$200 a night.

There were other people there who were of the same mindset as me. I became friends with Brent and Frank, who were also working at Old Faithful Lodge, and we started hanging out together after work. Brent was a piano player and had graduated from college with a music degree. He had been employed doing commercial jingles, and playing the clarinet and piano. He was taking a break from music, but felt Yellowstone might not be the place for him. I secretly had a crush on Brent; he was cute, smart, talented, and gay. He and Frank were thinking of going to Jackson Hole, Wyoming, thinking they might find a better summer job in that area since it was right in the Grand Teton Park. They asked me if I wanted to go. Of course I did, but I did not want to abandon Patty and the kids. Patty was lonely, as Gary was gone most of the week; I had just arrived there and Patty clearly was still excited about my coming to Mammoth to work. I told Brent and Frank to go and see what they could find and let me know.

Brent and Frank left for Jackson Hole, and within a week were back to tell me that Brent had landed a job as piano accompanist for the Jackson Hole Summer Stock Theatre doing *Fiddler on the Roof*. Frank was up for a possible role in the play, but had not yet heard if he got the part. They had come back for their belongings and would be leaving early the next morning; they asked if I wanted to go along. Although it was the hardest decision I had ever made in my life thus far and I felt terrible deserting Patty, for the first time in my life I acted selfishly and decided to go with Brent and Frank. Patty was disappointed and Mom was not happy with my decision at all. Brent, Frank, and I took off the next morning.

CHAPTER **10**

The Best Summer Ever

I REMEMBER BRENT and Frank watching me as we turned the corner in the car and the Grand Tetons seem to smack me square in the face. Both started to laugh as they watched my eyes grow wide with amazement and my mouth opened wide with astonishment. There was no warning that the Grand Tetons would be appearing. Pure unadulterated surprise and majesty, it was as if one had spoken and they appeared out of thin air. It was breathtaking; the sheer beauty of this mountain range was like nothing I had ever seen before, including Yellowstone and Glacier. I had a feeling I was going to like it here. I was wishing for a good summer.

We arrived at the theatre, where we got out and I started to take my things out of the car. Brent and Frank looked at each other and they seemed reluctant to speak about something. I asked what was going on. Frank told me there was a detail they had not told me as they figured it would be a temporary situation. It seemed that Brent was the only one with housing, since he was the only one who had been hired by the company for the play. I asked where we would be staying and Frank looked at Brent and started to laugh, a nervous laugh. He told me they had gotten a tent and we would be camping out until something opened up. I was silent—camping! Were they kidding? I hated camping. I was not the sleeping bag type of guy, and I needed a bed. This was not happening. With my fears and shock barely in check, we went into the theatre, and I was introduced to the cast of *Fiddler*.

I was rapidly dipped into the theatre culture, confronting a gregarious group, and witnessing a fluid intermingling among them. Ease among them was evident and their acceptance and positive freedom were so welcome. Without exception, they accepted me with no conditions, just as I was. If they had been a church, I would have joined right then and there. But there were no dues, no initiation rites, and no dogma that would have to be followed. I felt that there was an unwritten rule: Be yourself, John. I knew it was going to be a good summer.

Heading to the campsite, Frank asked me what I thought of the cast. I was smiling from ear to ear inside and was excited as I had ever been in my life, but I just replied I thought they were nice and looked forward to knowing them better. Entering the campsite I noticed it was an RV park, so that put me a little more at ease with the situation. Frank drove right up to where the tent was pitched and we got out, unloaded our belongings, and entered what would be our home for the next month. There were bathroom facilities, which included showers, so it was not as primitive as I had imagined. We had a Coleman camp stove to cook our meals, and a heater to take the bite out of the summer mountain air, which at night approached freezing. Frank had a few groceries, and we had pancakes for our first dinner in our tent.

For the next few weeks, Frank and I combed the area for any job openings. Since we had not been in the area at the start of the season, most of the good jobs were already taken; I began to second-guess leaving Yellowstone. After a couple of weeks, Frank informed me that he had gotten a job in Teton Village at a high-end restaurant. His sense of relief was palpable, only to be followed by news that the theatre company had offered him a part in *Fiddler* and he would be moving into the theatre housing. Self-pity and self-doubt kicked in. Not only would I be living alone in a tent, I had no transportation, no job, and no money— the perfect recipe for a great summer. I wondered how

SEEING THROUGH THE GLASS DARKLY

the Dirty Dancing group was faring and longed for a magical chance to turn back the clock. On the positive side, that weekend it poured rain and everything in the tent was soaked, and I was reminded how good I had it when the weather was fair. I was deeply depressed.

But as the sky cleared and opened to make known its heavenly presence, so did fate open up for me. Frank came over that Monday morning and told me since he had accepted the theatre's offer he could no longer work at Teton Village in the evenings. His boss offered him a position on the morning shift, but Frank, not being a morning person, declined. Thinking I might be able to take his position, he told his boss about me, but she had already had a guy for the evening post. She asked Frank if I might be interested in taking the morning shift, as she was having a hard time keeping people because of the early hours. Frank told me that Brent wanted to help and was offering his car for my transportation to and from Teton Village. I suspected that it was more than being a Good Samaritan for Brent, as there was a sexual tension between us. We were into each other.

I was ecstatic and went out to the Village to see my prospective boss. I arrived at the restaurant before 7:00 the next morning. Tina, the boss, arrived at 7:00 and seemed impressed that I was there waiting. We went through the boilerplate interview, and then she had me take her order and serve her breakfast. I passed and was told to start the next morning. I was to be there at 6:00 sharp. Working in Teton Village was the most fun I had ever had in a job. I worked with two very sweet young women, and we became very good friends over the next three months. Tina proved to be an outstanding boss. She was polite and courteous to her workers and she especially loved the morning help, as we gave her no grief or headaches, unlike the evening crew. Tina took care of us. If we had a tour bus, Tina would automatically add a 20% gratuity to their bill. Teton Village hosted many meetings of companies, sheiks from Arab countries, movie stars, and a wealthy class of people. Then there was the room service lottery. Many times the chef would fix hors d'oeuvres or a pastry platter and one of us three would have to take it up to the room.

THE BEST SUMMER EVER

We started flipping a coin to see who would be the lucky person, as it meant a 20% gratuity, which we did not have to share with the kitchen staff. Tina also gave us a free meal during each shift worked, unlike the evening crew, which was charged half price.

I began sending money home, a lot of money, more than what my parents expected I would be sending. I doubted myself no more and yes, my days as a depressed, soggy, pissed-off camper were behind me. My luck did not stop in getting a job in Teton Village. Soon afterward, one of the cast members quit *Fiddler*, and since the part was of the constable, with very few lines, Brent put a good word in for me. The head of casting called me in to audition for the part. I landed it. That would mean that I could also move into the theatre housing, and my meals would also be included. I was on a roll and I felt very blessed. Also, being associated with the theatre meant that I would be receiving a 25% discount from most stores in Jackson Hole. The community adored us and we were treated like royalty in Jackson Hole.

I grew close with many of the cast members, and my life that summer could not have been better. I had a great job, with great tips, and a great boss. I was having fun playing the role of the constable in *Fiddler*, and since I was able to live and eat as a cast member, I basically had no living expenses. All the money I was earning was essentially spending money, to do with as I wished. The majority I sent home to my parents, some I used to pay for my gas to get me to and from work, and the rest I had fun with.

One particular night we were on stage and during the segment when the constable hands the eviction notice to Tevye, he swung at the papers and missed. Tevye looked at me and he swung again for the papers and missed again. The audience was silent, probably thinking this was scripted. Tevye locked eyes with me and under his breath said, "Give me those fucking papers." Tevye, those around him, and I started to snicker, trying to keep a straight face. Tevye swung again and this time connected and was successful at taking them out of my hands. The show went on.

Supertramp's album *Breakfast in America* was extremely popular

SEEING THROUGH THE GLASS DARKLY

during the summer of my acting debut. The songs "Take the Long Way Home" and "The Logical Song" still take me back to Jackson Hole and my experience of that summer. So many lyrics from the songs seemed to describe my life. It did seem when I was younger my life indeed was feeling beautiful, magical. Then junior high and high school happened and I was bullied, assaulted, and was indeed the joke of the entire class. By the time I finished high school my life had become somewhat of a catastrophe. In hindsight I had been through numerous traumatic experiences. I understand now that this explains my lack of recollection for the events following my being dropped naked onto the floor of the girls' locker room: repression. The questions of "why" this was happening in my life were indeed running too deep for my simple mind; I had become cynical, disparaging and suspiciously questioning the motives of those who came in contact with me. But here I was on stage in front of an adoring audience, playing a role far different from the role of "Spud, the Ugly." This life I was experiencing that summer was unbelievable, so unforgettable how our audiences of Jackson Hole loved us. I felt, for the first time in my life, happy with who and what I was. And music was still my secret savior and confidante. I kept secrets tucked away in her songs, could work through private matters and problems discussed in her lyrics; I trusted her as none other.

I soon learned that most of the *Fiddler* cast was either gay or bisexual. They assumed I was gay and asked. I told them the truth as I knew it then: no I was not gay, I was straight. But why did I have this attraction toward Brent? This crush I felt for Brent scared me and I did not know how to handle this tension between us. I had never really thought about it before. From the age of thirteen I had been helping to raise children and working and fearing for my safety on a daily basis. The normal process of dating and coming to terms with my sexuality was not part of my adolescence of young adulthood. I was just so happy to be accepted by people that I really didn't care what I was. Nobody confronted me, but I feel they never really thought it was the truth, and they knew one day I would find out for myself. My just being John was good enough for them.

THE BEST SUMMER EVER

Surprise! The cast was quite flamboyant, style-conscious, and frolicking. They certainly knew how to draw attention. *The Rocky Horror Picture Show* was coming to town, playing at midnight, which meant the cast would be able to make it since *Fiddler* finished around 10:00. They asked if I wanted to accompany them and if I could get involved in doing the "props" for the movie. It was time for me to take *Rocky Horror 101*. After they told me the basics that one dresses as their favorite character from the show and one does certain "props" when mentioned in the movie, I agreed. It sounded like fun. I had no idea who the characters were, so they chose me to be the bride, including a wedding dress and flowers, Janet Wise. I was reluctant to go in drag, but they assured me everything would be fine and it was all in fun. So, having donned the wedding dress and my high heels, I was now ready for makeup. One of the girls put on my face—I looked into the mirror, and I looked *good*. We headed off to the show, where the line was a block long. Because we were from the theatre, they let us in the back door and we were all able to sit together since we were ahead of the crowd that was still outside. As a *Rocky Horror* virgin, I followed the lead of my friends, using the props at the appropriate times: rice, toast, flashlights, newspapers, water pistols; it went on and on. I'd never had so much fun at a movie before, and by the time it was over we were all wet, had rice in our hair and newsprint on our fingertips. We stumbled out of the theatre laughing, still doing the props at various stages. We started the walk home. Our group had split up, the majority going ahead while six of us lagged behind laughing and being silly.

We were taking our time and enjoying the warm August night. After about three blocks, we all felt a presence, which unfortunately I would feel many times again in my future, and we grew silent. Our pace quickened as we observed our surroundings. I was walking with Binky, one of the actresses, and she looked behind us. Binky told us not to turn around, as that would give us away and we would probably not get home safely. My heart started to quicken, as did my walking. There were approximately ten men behind us, late adolescents and young adults. They were locals, cowboys. Suffice it to say that these guys were not walking home from a Western-themed gay bar. From the tone of Binky's voice and the imposing gang they represented, things were not looking favorable. They were all business. Binky told me to take my high heels off so I could run faster. She told the other four at her signal of "Go!" to split up and go to the 24-hour restaurant; Binky and I would try to make it to the theatre. In doing this, she reasoned it would split their group up. Divide and conquer. My anxiety skyrocketed as I waited for Binky's command, heels in hand, dress pulled up. Jesus, what had I gotten into? Binky softly gave the signal and we all sprinted our separate ways.

With Jackson Hole having so many boardwalks to go along with the town's Western theme, running was not that easy, with the divisions in between the boards. If they were hurting my bare feet, I did not feel the pain. Adrenaline had kicked in, and I just wanted to get to the theatre without any blood on my wedding dress. We saw the theatre one block away and started screaming for whoever was there to please hear us and open the doors. We screamed louder as we approached, and someone came out. As they heard us screaming for them to get back in, they saw what was happening and went back inside, waiting for us to enter. They slammed and locked the door behind us. Out of breath, we tried telling them what had transpired, and that four of our family were at the restaurant where we assumed the cowboys would be headed. It was time to round up the troops and go protect our own. I quickly changed and wiped the makeup off of my face.

The rest of the cast was notified; we assembled in the lobby, and then headed toward the restaurant. Running toward the restaurant, we made it in about ten minutes. The four from whom we had parted company while running from the cowboys were there, looking nervous. The cowboys were already there, surrounding their table. Binky took the lead and crowded between the cowboys, and pulled up a table to join the lone four. Being female, Binky got away with this; no cowboy would ever hit a woman. The females of the cast took their cue from Binky and kept adding tables; the males quietly joining after the tables were together. Soon we had a table of twenty, outnumbering the cowboys. Binky saw one of the cowboys leave and she leaned over and whispered that she thought he was going for backup. Within fifteen minutes he was back with another dozen guys. It was evident they were going to beat the shit out of us. I called over the waitress and in a soft voice told her she had better call the police, as I believed we were in danger and it would be only a short while until their anger would turn violent. Within five minutes the police came, each side told their version of the story, and the police escorted the cowboys from the restaurant, off to jail.

For the remainder of the summer, members of our cast did not go anywhere without a companion. It was too dangerous, and our manager insisted that we all adhere to this one rule, no exceptions. This was my first witnessing of what society would later refer to as a potential for a "hate crime." Although I had experienced this hate and violence toward me during my school years, I had never seen it directed at another person. Years later, when Matthew Shepard would make the news for being tortured and murdered in Laramie, because of his sexual orientation, I was not surprised it took place in Wyoming. I view Wyoming as being very homophobic, with more than its fair share of American ignorance and intolerance. Was it ignorance, or plain stupidity, with no chance for remediation or change? I had seen it before in Montana, and this bought back all those painful memories. I saw all those people of my past as bullies—and sadly I was not big enough to try to find a solution for their stupidity. Perhaps they were the ones who were being short-changed. Perhaps their creator did not give them the capacity for empathy, to recognize feelings that are uniquely human. Perhaps one day love would help them all to overcome their stupidity and hatred. Perhaps I was the one who was stupid; perhaps I did not have empathy for their shortcomings; perhaps I was the one who was filled with hatred. I did not like where my mind was taking me.

We ended the summer by celebrating Christmas in August. Since we probably would not be together for Christmas it was tradition that summer stock celebrate Christmas early. We went to the mountains, chopped down a tree, brought it back to the theatre, and decorated it in the lobby before our last presentation of *Fiddler*. We each drew names and bought a gift as a Secret Santa. I purchased additional gifts, as I felt very close to almost the whole crew. I was getting sad thinking about leaving my friends at the theatre, and also at Teton Village.

Much like Supertramp's song "Goodbye Stranger," on that last day I was up before the dawn, as I wanted to spend as much time as I could with my friends before my mom and Patty came to take me back to Lewistown. The company had tried talking me into going to Hawaii, where they would be putting on a production of *Snow White*. I was so tempted, but Dad's health was fragile, and I felt I would be needed at home. I had really enjoyed my stay, but much like the song, I had to be moving on to my responsibilities back home. My time in Jackson Hole had drawn to a close—and as I had hoped it would be, it was the best summer in my life. I was indeed blessed to have known these people, albeit for a short time, but a critical time, during which my identity was finally beginning to take root, among the most beautiful of mountains and the most precious of memories. I sat silent all the way home, my eyes tearing up thinking of what I was leaving and what was awaiting me.

When I want to go back to that special time in my life I just put Supertramp on, close my eyes and fumble through all those files in my mind, and I am immediately there, along with all the feelings I had at that time, with all my friends again—and I smile. Yes, it was my best summer ever.

CHAPTER **11**

It's Raining Again

SUPERTRAMP'S SONG "IT'S Raining Again" captures how I was feeling going back once again to Lewistown. It was raining in my heart and I was missing my friends. But like the song, I had to be the fighter and get back up again; no need to be uptight about my situation. *Dear Abby*, after all, almost always said it would get better; I was back to my mantra, "It will get better," "It will get better." Little did I know that a mantra can be self-deceptive. More than a decade had passed since Dad had a massive heart attack that pretty much blew his left ventricle wide open; doctors said he would never make it through that night. But he did, in large part; I am certain, due to my mother. My mom would sneak large doses of Vitamin E into Dad's hospital room, and, when the nurses were not looking, would have Dad take them. My mom was always reading and she was reading a lot about supplements at a time when they were not yet accepted or popular, especially within the medical professions. So, whatever the reason, Dad was still around and I was thankful, but Dad had congestive heart failure, he was tired, nearing seventy, had lost a son, was no longer able to work, and was watching more and more of his friends die. The next three years would be a harrowing rollercoaster for Mom and me.

I was working at the Fergus Café again as a server (yes, I was putting my college business degree to good use) and had purchased a home right next door to my parents. This would prove to be invaluable over the next five years, relative to being close to Dad, during a time when he would start a series of multiple hospitalizations. Dad would enter the hospital for a period of usually two to three weeks. Then if we were lucky, he would be able to stay out for close to a month— if really lucky, six weeks. As with my brother Billy, when he entered the hospital, Mom was steadfast and loving in her devotion. She took her marriage vows seriously and, in health and sickness, she stood by my father. I believe that witnessing these acts of devotion, commitment, and purpose of resolution in trying to solve the mystery of betrayal by my dad's body had a very positive effect on my character. My mother's selflessness for the family's good would have both positive and negative effects on my life, as it had already.

After getting off my morning shifts at the Fergus Café, I would take Mom back up to the hospital. She had already been there and back home, walking close to a three-mile round trip to visit him. Mom and I would stay until visiting hours ended at 9:00 p.m., then back home, with a repeat the next day. During the weekends we would stay there pretty much the whole day, coming home only to check the mail, grab a bite to eat, and enjoy a short break. This we did for close to three years. I remember one sunny July weekend, we were once again at the hospital, keeping Dad company, and I was feeling sorry for myself. Mom asked me what was wrong and I blurted out that I wanted to be out with my friends, but I had to be here. Immediately I wished I could have taken those hurtful words back, I felt horrible. Mom and Dad said nothing; I said nothing. I was deeply ashamed. Dad just looked out the window staring, his heart breaking further, I'm sure, not from the disease but from his son's insensitivity.

We left early that night and when we got into the car, Mom told me she never wanted to hear anything like that out of my mouth again. She told me that Dad was dying and she did not want me to have to deal with the pain that words that I had just spoken would bring me later on. Mom told me not to leave it like that, to go back into the hospital and tell Dad I was sorry. I did as Mom requested and in the process broke down and cried. I loved my dad and was just tired—tired of the sickness, the mundane routine, the prison that his sickness had put us in. But Mom was right; I would have to deal with the guilt later on if I did not make this right before day's end. Dad also broke down, but I believe he was thankful that I came back in and made things right, or at least as right as I could. Valuable lesson: I was a lucky son to have such good teachers in life.

My mom said she would never put Dad in a nursing home, but laws concerning hospital bills and who would pay for what, whether it be Medicare or Medicaid and what they would and would not pay for won out in the end. Dad needed around-the-clock care toward the last year of his life. Mom would have done it, but again he needed medical care that she could not provide. Dad could not stay in the hospital; his premiums had run out, so the only option available was a nursing home. Mom hated that decision, but she had no choice if she wanted to keep Dad alive. So he entered the nursing home fully aware, and I could see a distinct change in his face and in his eyes. He was coming to terms with his mortality. I am sure he was very depressed and sad, although he never expressed it. Dad would stay in the nursing home and, when his condition warranted it, would enter ICU. The last time he entered ICU, my nurse friend called me at my house around midnight. Mom and I had returned from the hospital around 10:00 p.m., so I had been in bed for approximately an hour when I was awakened by the phone ringing. Reaching the phone in fear, expecting to hear Mom's voice, I was surprised to hear my friend's voice on the other end. She calmed my fear immediately and told me Dad was fine. But she thought that Dad would benefit if I came back to the hospital, because he was crying and asking for me.

I arrived to find Dad crying and shaking. My friend nodded at me to assure me and I sat on his bed. I asked Dad what was going on and he answered, "Johnny, I'm just so afraid of dying; I don't want to leave you and Mom."

I was twenty-six years of age, and I had no wisdom stored up yet—at least none that I thought would help my father. Yes, death and dying I had experienced, but I certainly was not wise enough to help my father in this unknown world he would more than likely be entering in the very near future. During our interaction, Dad had a bowel movement and the nurse came in to clean him up. I told her I would clean him up and, in fact, insisted when she said I couldn't because of regulations. Because she was my friend, and my dad was the only one in the ICU, I believe she made an exception. I cleaned Dad with gentleness and dignity, thinking back to all he had given me in my life. After I changed him, he calmed down and he thanked me. I sat back down on his bed again and he told me he was indeed lucky to have a good son like me. He proceeded to tell me he was proud of me and loved me and when he died to take care of his "Sugar Foot," his term of endearment for my mother. I promised him I would, but told him he did not have to think about that because he was going to be around for a long time. I knew I was lying, but I did not want to confront reality, and it was all I had to give him—false reassurance.

CHAPTER **12**

Now It's Pouring

WE HAD MADE it through the holidays, and although Dad was not able to spend that last Thanksgiving at home, we were lucky enough to have him spend Christmas with us. We knew it would probably be Dad's last Christmas, and we approached it with the same machinations as any other holiday. If we had tried to make it special or different, that would have been a very clear indication into our thoughts of the future, and we did not want Dad to pick up on any of our fears. Tradition and predictability ruled. By this time, Dad was very weak and had lost much of his healthy weight. Shortly after the New Year, Dad entered the hospital for the last time, and subsequently the nursing home followed. Mom and I had reverted to our schedule once again, Mom walking to the hospital while I worked the morning shift at the café. After work I would meet Mom at home, where we would take off again for the hospital, where we would stay with Dad until visiting hours were over at 9:00. Then back home, where we would go to our separate homes and bedtime; back up again by 5:00 a.m. to start the same schedule all over again.

Shortly after we had admitted Dad into the hospital that New Year, a twist entered our lives. That Wednesday following the holiday, my shift had not yet ended at the café when Mom walked in with my sister Patty's four kids. Seeing them walk in, I had a puzzled look on my face, as Patty and the kids had just gone back to Yellowstone

◄ SEEING THROUGH THE GLASS DARKLY

a few days earlier and nothing seemed to be out of the ordinary. I looked at Mom with questioning eyes; Mom just shook her head and sat down with the kids in my section. Mom proceeded to tell me that Patty had decided to end her marriage to her husband Gary and had bundled the kids up and bought them with her to Lewistown. Patty had decided that she had had enough of Gary's controlling behavior and wanted a life that included friends and fun. She was getting back together with her friends from high school—the same friends that she got into trouble with when she was a teenager. Mom told her to leave the kids at the house, as she knew that this decision of Patty's would only jeopardize the children's welfare.

I was stunned. I knew that Gary was controlling and did not like Patty having any friends around when he was home, but I had no idea that their relationship had gotten so bad. Patty leaving Gary, I could understand. No one likes loneliness and being isolated from others. Patty was a social animal and enjoyed having people around her; this I could fully understand. It was how she proceeded with a plan that included putting her life first and her children's lives second that I struggled with. Patty essentially was dropping the responsibility for her children into Mom's and my laps, at a time when our plates were very full with Dad's failing health.

I ended my shift in about thirty minutes and all of us walked home, Mom filling me in with more details on the way there. We got the kids home and proceeded to follow our hospital routine, as we had for the past three years now. We put coloring books, puzzles, etc. into a bag for the kids and packed a supper for all of us, which we would supplement with items from the hospital's cafeteria. Once we arrived at the hospital, we found a waiting room where the kids could do their activities and watch television while Mom and I visited Dad. The kids, being minors, were not allowed into Dad's room. We did not stay until 9:00 that night, as we had to get home and figure out where the kids would be sleeping, and Patty's plans, if any, for the kids' schooling. Maybe this was just a temporary thing; perhaps Patty would get this resentment and anger for Gary out of her system and

NOW IT'S POURING

go back home to him. There were so many unknowns, and still a lot of questions that were not yet answered. It was decided that the kids would stay at Mom's house, as that was the only logical choice since I went to work so early each morning. We had no idea where Patty had gone or where she was staying the night.

The next day, Mom and Patty had further conversations and arguments about the situation, and it was decided that the kids would be enrolling into the Lewistown School District. That Thursday afternoon, Mom and I took the children and enrolled them into first, second, sixth, and seventh grades. It involved only two different schools, so at least that was some help, and the schools were close enough that as the kids got more familiar with Lewistown, they would be able to walk to school. Mom would have to walk them all to school for the first few days.

The days that followed turned worse. Mom tried to reason with Patty in returning to Gary and trying to work things out, if not for themselves, then for the children, but Patty would have none of that. Mom then tried to reason with Patty that if she was going to divorce Gary, to at least stay with her kids and forget her friends. Again Patty said it was time for her to be happy and she was going to have her "fun." Given that this was Patty, this meant alcohol, drugs, and a steady stream of being AWOL. And so it was that my life and my mother's were about to change dramatically and would never be the same again. With Dad being so ill, my sister Mary decided to come back home to Lewistown for a short while. This did not help. Both my sisters started to drink and do drugs, even selling drugs, all the time while Dad was dying. There started to be interactions with the police again, and trouble at school with Patty picking up the kids while intoxicated. Mom and I continued our visits to Dad at the nursing home, bringing the kids with us each night except for that rare circumstance when Patty would have the kids, leaving Mom and me fearful of what might transpire because of her penchant for her "fun." What we feared most was Family Services being called in to investigate and the kids possibly being taken from Patty's custody and placed

SEEING THROUGH THE GLASS DARKLY

in foster care. Mom was not going to let that happen. There would be ugly fights between Mom and Patty, but almost always Mom would win out and for another day the kids would remain safe, far from the hands of Family Services.

The year 1984 proved to be a most devastating year for our family. Before the year's end, death's scythe would claim nine members of our family: my father, and numerous aunts and uncles. I remember my Uncle Jimmy being admitted to the hospital with a case of possible exposure from toxins used for weed control. Both my mom and I would go from Dad's room to the waiting room where other aunts, uncles, and cousins were gathering awaiting news about Uncle Jimmy. Jimmy was one of my favorite uncles, and he was dead within three days. I was asked to speak at his funeral service. Mom could not attend her brother's funeral, as Dad was very bad and we did not know if Dad would make it while she attended Jimmy's funeral. At his funeral, I got up to speak, looked out into the crowd, and started to read the words I had written down. I became overwhelmed with emotion; I choked and broke down crying. Those sitting in the pews knew what was going on and although there was silence, I felt a strength coming from my family—my cousins, uncles, aunts. My favorite cousin came to the podium and stood by me as I read in honor of Uncle's Jimmy's memory. This was too much; I pictured myself in replay in the very near future, although this next time it would be for my father.

Easter was now nearing and I remember people bringing food, cakes, and flowers over to our house. There were expressions of hope that whatever they offered might help us to get through this sacred holiday and somehow keep our faith strong that God was still good and whatever He had planned for our family was for the best. I appreciated their caring gestures, but I really did not care what God was planning or what He was thinking. All I knew was that I was sad and tired. The Mom and John routine now comfortably included the kids, even though it was more work. I would help the kids with any homework they might have while they were in the waiting room while we were visiting Dad. Dad's time was getting very close. The

NOW IT'S POURING

Friday following Easter, we had done our usual routine and we knew that Dad's body was shutting down. I had taken off of work and had been at the hospital all day, except to get the kids after they got home from school and bring them up to the hospital. Having not eaten all day, I was tired and hungry. Mom suggested that I go to the cafeteria and grab a bite. I was reluctant to leave Dad but thought if I hurried, it would probably be okay. I decided to go, and told them to come and get me if anything started to change.

I went to the cafeteria, purchased some food, sat down at a table, and closed my eyes, thinking of the day, thinking of Dad, and thinking of what would probably happen before day's end. I heard the sound of someone running down the hall; I looked up and saw Mary. Before getting to my table she started shouting at me to hurry and come back to Dad's room—something was happening and I should come back immediately. We both ran back to Dad's room and as we entered, everyone was crying. Dad was gone. I looked at everyone, asking what had happened as if I had not a clue what had just transpired. My cousin Betty told me that Dad had just passed. I began crying, stating that I should not have left, I should have stayed, it was selfish of me to think about eating when Dad was so ill. Betty told me not to be silly, that I had been with him nonstop for the last three years; I had given my dad all the love a son could give a dad, and I should not feel bad about anything. Betty's words did not help. My guilt started to consume me; I kept thinking how weak and selfish I was that I could not wait a few minutes longer to be with my dad when he passed. Then anger surfaced. Why did others in my family have the privilege to be with my dad in his passing when they did not spend anywhere near the time that Mom and I had spent with him the past three years? It was not fair; I had been short-changed by God, and it was almost as if a cruel joke had been played on me. I had put my time in only to be denied that final reward, to be with Dad when he passed, to hold his hand, and for him to be aware that I was still there—that I had stayed the course, I had not faltered.

But falter I did, and had stumbled at the very last moment of this

SEEING THROUGH THE GLASS DARKLY

long walk with my father, and I was not able to get my balance and step back on to that road to let him know that I was still there for him, carrying him along with Mom as he entered a new world. Others were given that privilege of ushering him gently into that unknown. I vowed to never let that happen again with a loved one, and the anger inside me grew. It was at this time that I started hating holidays; nothing good would ever come out of them. The first holiday on that list would be Easter, and the list would grow. For the final time, I leaned over and whispered to my father. I thanked him for being the dad he was for me—loving, caring, gentle, strong, and giving of his time. I was indeed a very lucky son.

CHAPTER 13

Life Goes On

AFTER DAD'S DEATH, I felt I had been kicked in the stomach—that a piece of my heart was missing. I would learn that each death in my immediate family would be harder than the last. Life went on, not because we wanted it to go on but because it just did; we had no say in the matter. Patty's kids learned that death was a part of life, and while taking the kids to see their grandpa one more time, Mom and I were taught that even in death, there can be funny moments. Mom wanted the kids to see their grandpa one more time and felt they needed closure. Otherwise, death might seem mysterious and even scary to them. She did not believe that children were ever too young to learn about dying, or that it might scar them if they were confronted with death at too early an age. She was an intelligent and insightful woman, even though she didn't have a high school education. We took the children to the funeral home that Sunday night, and while they were viewing their grandpa's body one last time, Shane took his finger and poked Dad in the face. He pulled it back and said: "Oh my God, Grandpa feels like a rubber Grandpa!" I looked at Mom and we both started to laugh, with the kids soon joining in. What a good memory Shane gave to us all—and what a good lesson that even in death there are lighter moments.

It was as if an invisible hand reached down from the heavens and put our gears in automatic drive—we did not have to shift gears to move on with life; we just had to steer our lives so that we did not collide with any oncoming event in our future. We had gotten through two of the nine deaths that the family would incur in 1984. Most of the deaths were on my mom's side of the family. Mom's parents had sixteen children, many very close in age, so I guess it was pretty much in the statistics that deaths would occur just as fast as their births did, but that year it seemed that our family was having a pile-up on life's freeway. Every time the phone would ring we were reluctant to answer, scared of what the message coming through the wires might be. Life had its own medication for the pain that we were feeling in our hearts—numbness. As death marched forward on his journey, so also did our lives.

I feel that we actually never were able to mourn Dad's death in a proper manner. Within weeks there was another death, and sorrow was yet again divided. This experience gave me a glimpse into what the dying must feel. Not only are they losing their own life, but they must say goodbye to everyone else, be they a loved one, acquaintance, or an enemy. What a burden, and what a sorrow they must feel both in mind and heart. And then there was the situation with my two sisters and the four children. This situation was like a slap in the face, a wake-up call telling us to snap out of it. Yes, we were experiencing deaths, but four very young innocent lives were depending on us and we had to steer our lives so that we did not have any major incidents that might potentially harm the children's welfare, as their future was already questionable. This was no time for self-pity.

Mom would try reasoning with Patty about the kids, but alcohol and drugs were clouding Patty's judgment. Mom was nearing seventy and did not want to have to raise another family. I did not want to help Mom raise another family. I had helped Patty with the kids since I was thirteen. I had done my part, and I certainly did not want that responsibility either. We turned to Patty's husband, Gary. He was the father of the two boys, and although he was controlling, he seemed to be a loving, caring father to the boys and seemed to treat the girls as if they too were his own. So during the course of that summer, Gary would come down from Yellowstone on the weekends to discuss the children's ultimate placement. He told Mom that he would be able to get family housing in West Yellowstone so the kids would be able to attend school there, and life could resume as before. During one of his visits, I noticed Gary speaking to Charlee. I watched, interested in their interaction. Suddenly Charlee seemed very upset with Gary and yelled at him. I immediately reprimanded Charlee, scolding her and shaming her by telling her that Gary was only trying to help the family. That was a low point for me as an uncle, as I impulsively rebuked my lovely fourteen-year-old niece who, we would learn, shared a dark secret with Gary. It never occurred to me to simply ask Charlee why she seemed so angry with him.

So the decision was made, and we would start the children's placement, splitting up their time gradually between Mammoth and Lewistown. That following Friday night we got the kids in the car and started the three-hour trip to West Yellowstone. We arrived around 9:00 and Gary was still working. A red flag was being thrown up: would Gary be able to work his schedule and provide proper supervision to the kids? Gary assured us that he would be able to accommodate the children into an amended schedule. He really wanted the children and assured us that they were the number-one priority in his life. We could stay only until Sunday evening, as my shift at the café started at 6:00 the next morning. We said our goodbyes to the children, got into the car, and I started to pull out.

As we started to back out of the driveway, Mom told me to stop. I stopped and through the windshield saw Charlee at the window, clutching the curtains with her left hand as her right hand waved goodbye. She was crying, and I assumed it was because she was sad to see us leave. Mom's intuition told her something very different. She felt uneasy and asked me if I thought we should go back in and take the children back home with us. I assured her that everything was fine, that Charlee was crying because she was especially close to her Grandma. I told her that if this placement with Gary was to work, we had to give it a chance. Mom reluctantly agreed. We headed back to

SEEING THROUGH THE GLASS DARKLY

Lewistown, while Mom's intuition spilled out as she enumerated her concerns about the children.

That following Friday, as soon as my shift was done at the café, Mom had everything packed into the car for our trip back to West Yellowstone to pick up the kids. It was our turn to have the kids for a week and Mom was anxious to get them back to Lewistown. She had been uneasy and worried all week. Mom had even talked to Marilyn, Leland's wife, hinting at the unthinkable.

Marilyn and I never really hit it off, failing to see eye to eye on many things. Once while visiting Leland and her in Miles City, Marilyn had prepared dinner for Mary and me. The main course was beef, which Mary and I ate without hesitation, except that on my plate there was this sizeable chunk of pure fat. Now fat is something I hate with a nauseating passion. I have gagged even on small pieces of animal fat. To this day, Marilyn swears it was venison, but I believe it was beef fat. Mary was excused from the table, as her plate was empty. I was not excused because my plate still had "food" on it. I tried to reason with Marilyn that this was not food; it was fat, not part of any food group. Marilyn told me that I could get up from the table just as soon as I "cleaned my plate." The battle was on. It lasted three hours, and then I gave in, swallowing small bits of "venison" with water, choking and gagging. Marilyn had a smile on her face. She won this battle, but I was determined to win the war.

Friday night came, Leland had returned home from work, and we were headed back to Lewistown. For some reason, Marvin and his wife Bernice were also there, and we would all be traveling back in the same car. On the way back to Lewistown, we had not yet eaten supper and Marvin knew that our parents would ask if we had had supper yet. He told me and Mary to say yes so they would not have to prepare us a meal. We agreed. We arrived in Lewistown around 8:00 and I ran in the house and hugged Mom and Dad. The first question out of Mom's mouth: "Have you had supper yet?" I very purposefully looked both Marvin and Marilyn in the eye as I responded: "No, I'm hungry." I won this battle, and I was smiling. The war with Marilyn

LIFE GOES ON

would take years to play out. It ended in a cease-fire as I got to know her better. Marilyn was a Montana version of a New Jersey girl—edgy, quick-witted, streetwise, and a loving mother.

We arrived in West Yellowstone around 6:00 that night. All the kids rushed to give us a hug and Charlee held on to Mom longer and tighter than usual. I knew that Charlee had a much closer bond to her grandmother than the other kids, but I was starting to see something else, and it was starting to scare me. We stayed overnight and, the next morning, Mom made up an excuse that we needed to get back to Lewistown that day. Gary did not seem upset with Mom's excuse and seemed to be actually relieved that he would not be tending to the kids for the next week. So off to Lewistown we went. For the remainder of the weekend we just hung out with the kids and made sure everything was low-key for them. That Monday, Mom took Charlee aside and asked her about life with Gary, and how it was living in Yellowstone. Charlee seemed evasive and Mom believed that Charlee was scared, that perhaps she was too close to her granddaughter and would feel more at ease with someone else. Mom telephoned Marilyn and asked if she could talk to Charlee. Mom's radar was going haywire, and maybe Charlee would confide in Marilyn.

Charlee eventually told Marilyn that Gary had been sexually abusing her, and perhaps the other children. Mom suspected this ever since seeing Charlee clutching the curtain as I backed out of the driveway. Mom decided that the kids would be staying with her permanently. She telephone Gary to inform him of her decision, not to dare fight her on it, and that she would be getting the authorities involved. She was coming after him. She also decided to file for temporary custody of the children, given that Patty was often AWOL and still hopped up on her addictions.

My role would evolve to be not only the father figure, but the disciplinarian as well. I had always been more than an uncle to Patty's kids, more like a surrogate father. I would come to resent this more formal role that I had been placed in. I felt the kids, especially Shawn, resented both Mom and me for replacing their parents, for seemingly coming in between them and their mother. I was twenty-six years old and was probably not the best candidate for this position, but it was one of necessity. I would make many mistakes in my efforts to raise the kids, but I loved them dearly. Those mistakes I would make I must look beyond, and I hope the kids would also.

The remainder of the summer was spent at the district attorney's office, trying to make a case against Gary. Since state lines had been crossed when the abuse took place, the DA's office thought perhaps the FBI might be able to get involved as well. I believed that never happened and, in the end, no charges were filed against Gary. It was understood that he would never attempt to get custody of the children, even his boys. His parental rights were never terminated legally, and many years later he would fall to his death while rock climbing.

That Indian summer the kids entered the Lewistown schools for the second time and it was during that autumn that I got a glimpse into my mother's own heartache. She had just lost her husband of forty-five years, lost numerous sisters and brothers, and now, entering her 70s, she was responsible for four young children. She had to do her grieving in between preparing meals, washing clothes, keeping watch, and just being exhausted. Her life had been rebooted, and little did we know that the motherboard was about to crash.

CHAPTER **14**

Another Life

ENTER STAGE LEFT: Mary and her boyfriend Gary. Gary 2.0…perhaps this one would be more human and not so destructive. They decided to move to Lewistown from Nebraska and to help me do some renovations on my house. Their help was "free." All I had to do was pay for the materials. This was a big mistake on my part. You get what you pay for, right? Mary and Gary did not know what they were doing, even though they owned a construction company. Their work was painstakingly slow and shoddy. They were getting free room and board and I was getting a house renovation that would not pass inspections. Mom and I accepted Gary as best we could. He was of slender build, had long unkempt hair, was exceedingly lazy (loved to go fishing instead of working), and had a drug problem. He and Mary both drank too much and were addicted to coc and meth. Smoking pot was the least of their problems. Leland took an immediate dislike to Gary, once pointing out to me everything that was wrong with the guy. Looking back on that conversation, I wish I had given more credence to his words and warnings. I think I was wishing against that persistent nagging in my voice that this Gary could not be as bad as the last one. It's like I was the one on drugs and in denial.

Then the big announcement came: Mary and Gary were getting married! Mom took the news as if she just learned that she would need experimental oral surgery. But it was her daughter and she quietly made the best of it. Leland was not quiet. "Kernal" had a special place in his heart. He spoke up in protest, calling the planned marriage a mistake, predicting that it would not last, and vehemently proclaiming that the marriage would be a cover for symbiotic enabling of each other's drug and alcohol addictions. Leland spoke forthrightly, but he might as well have been talking to an old chair. The marriage would take place in Mom's back yard and Gary's family would be traveling from Nebraska to attend. Where would the groom's family stay? Mom took it upon herself to offer Leland and Marilyn's house as that place.

This presented a small problem to Leland and Marilyn. They felt Mom had overstepped her boundaries in offering up their house. They were not in agreement with the marriage plans, and it was their house, and they should have a say who was to be their guests. Leland acted as referee between his mother and his wife. He had a talk with Mom and told her that because she had already offered their house they would honor it, but never to let it happen again. He made it very clear that this was their decision and she had no say in the matter. It was one of a very few times that our mother was ever confronted. This was hard for Mom to swallow, but I believe that deep down she knew they were right. I believe that Mom was at her wits' end and she was taking the easiest road out of a difficult and complicated issue.

Soon after the wedding, a local grocery store caught on fire and was destroyed. Mary and Gary saw an opportunity, and I was a part of it. They reasoned that if they were able to get the building for a discount they could restore it and open up a restaurant. The Fergus Café was about to have its doors closed by the IRS, so that inventory could be transferred to the new restaurant. My experience working at different restaurants, and with scheduling and inventory, could prove invaluable. Gary had money coming from an inheritance that he felt he could borrow on, and I was asked if I could also contribute. So the stage was set, and soon Mary and Gary had negotiated a price for the building. Gary borrowed on his inheritance, and I gave also. It was a rag-tag set of misfits that Mary used in the revamping of the old grocery store into a restaurant. Have drugs, will renovate. Thank God we had our brother Leland helping us; otherwise, its doors would never have opened. Leland was skillful with his hands and he had vision. Every weekend he would be at the restaurant helping us renovate—never asking for money, he did it out of love. Mom's part in this new venture was providing lunch every day for these misfits.

Because Mary and Gary were already mishandling the inheritance to feed their drug habits, we feared losing our shirts in the process. We did whatever we could do to hold on to the misfits. Both Gary and Mary would have dealers coming to the restaurant to sell them drugs, financed by the money that was supposed to be for the restaurant. I, in the meantime, was trying to keep this ship afloat and had maxed out all my credit cards, making the proverbial "minimum payment" on all of them. I had also put my car up as collateral to one of the building suppliers. Talk about enabling! Mom and I were at the top of the list every step of the way. We did not see it then—out of fear, I guess. This happens in families with addictions. But when I look back at these events, I shake my head in disbelief and ask myself, "Were you absolutely crazy?"

The restaurant opened and was very popular for a very short time. Payroll—with all the taxes, unemployment, and Social Security—started to put a strain on the business, and we had to cut back on the help. Since Gary was not working, he was supposed to take one of the cook shifts. I came by one afternoon to find angry customers who were waiting for their meals for well over an hour. Seems Gary had taken off to do some fishing. He did not tell anyone that he was going. He later told me that because he was the owner, he did not have to explain his actions to anyone, certainly not to me. That gave me a clue as to just how messed-up his mind was with drugs. Did he think that our customers would put up with irresponsibility and the irrational reasoning that he was using to justify his actions? Rumors started to circulate that the restaurant was a façade for drug transactions. We were not going to make it.

On cue, as if a hack Hollywood screenwriter was running our lives, Mary then announced that she was pregnant. Instantly, as I

◂ SEEING THROUGH THE GLASS DARKLY

stood there, I felt as if someone had kicked me in the stomach; I literally felt sick. I did not want another child to care for. Anyone reading this might think it presumptuous of me to think along these lines, but considering Mary's and Gary's lack of parental skills, immaturity, and their drug problems, I would beg to differ. I went out of the restaurant to catch my breath. I was shaking, my heart was racing; this could not be happening. Gary had literally and figuratively "Gone Fishin'," and now drug-addicted Mary was pregnant. What had I done in a past life to warrant these cruel jokes on children, on me? I thought I was a decent person, but I must have been a most vile, despicable, wretchedly horrible being to keep being assaulted with all this shit that life was throwing at me. Let me not forget about my mother—what type of person had she been in her past life? Obviously we had been partners in our past and had flung much shit ourselves at others who were not deserving of it. And if one believes in karma, as I do, this was payback. I just wish I could understand, lest I forget, and the same shit would be recycled yet again to be hurled at us in another life.

About six months into Mary's pregnancy, Mom asked me to go with her to a doctor's appointment. Mom had been having health problems, had undergone a partial hysterectomy a year earlier, and had been having spot bleeding off and on. I assumed that she might have ulcers due to all the stress in her life. The appointment was for that afternoon and I remember sitting in the doctor's office while the doctor was speaking to Mom telling her that he thought I should be told. I looked at Mom with that puzzled look on my face that I had given her many times in my life when I did not fully understand. Told what? That Mom had an ulcer and that is why her stomach was the size of a baseball bulging outward when it used to be so flat? Why was the doctor making such a big issue of this? Denial.

Mom looked at the doctor and replied "Yes, I guess he should be told."

Mom looked into my eyes while the doctor said, "Your mom has ovarian cancer."

The only word I heard was cancer. Cancer! I teared up and I

choked as I started to speak. "Cancer, how could this be, are you sure?"

The doctor was silent, looking into my mother's tearful eyes. The cruelest joke yet.

We drove home in silence. Back at the house, each member of the family was called and they started to trickle into the house and assemble around Mom. We each gave our pep talk to her and to one another, trying to calm fears and put some brakes on racing thoughts and fantasies of a slow, painful dying process. To me these thoughts were more than imagination, based on our recent string of losses, Gary 1.0 being a molester, and Gary 2.0 an unspeakably irresponsible guy obsessed with drug-fueled fishing…seriously bad karma. My heart was heavy and I did not know it at that time, but I was starting the grieving process for my mom before her death; pre-emptive mourning. I had always been a momma's boy and the thought of losing her overwhelmed and paralyzed me with fear of the unknown. The unknown was so many things: the children's welfare, the troubles between myself and my sisters, the restaurant, my troubled financial condition, and yet another child on the way—as if Mary was serving as a surrogate for my next child.

I learned that Mom's cancer was probably the result of her partial hysterectomy. Had she gotten a complete hysterectomy along with an oophorectomy (removal of the ovaries) her chances of getting ovarian cancer would have been greatly reduced. At the time, a partial hysterectomy was all that was allowed under the Medicare guidelines. Had I known, I would have gladly paid for the other procedures to be performed. I now had guilt to go along with my sorrow.

It was decided that Mom and the kids should move in with me, a strategic move on Mom's part to prepare for the inevitable future. I would take more of a role with the kids' upbringing and increasingly help Mom as her health quickly worsened. The restaurant proved to be a huge help, in that we ate all of our meals there, and it took a big burden off of both Mom and me in preparing meals. Since we were not receiving any income from the restaurant, at least we received meals. Any money that the restaurant did generate was quickly taken by Mary or Gary, depending on who would get there first. My debt started to mount and I was unable to pay my bills for the first time in my life. I needed to find another job fast, and went searching.

I applied at the local grocery store, Buttrey, a small chain with stores in Montana, Wyoming, and North Dakota. I told Louie, the manager, that I would do anything, I just needed a job. Louie took my words literally and had me clean out the incinerator. I did not hesitate, jumped in, and did the cleaning as best I could. I wanted to make a good impression on Louie; I wanted him to know that I was a good worker. By the time I was done cleaning the incinerator I was covered in soot. I went to tell Louie I was done. Looking at me he smiled, told me to go home and get cleaned up, then come back and we would talk. I came back that same afternoon and Louie asked me if I would be interested in a position as a bagger. I jumped at the chance and expressed my gratitude to him. My work ethic and lessons from my parents served me well, as Louie kept promoting me: to checker, produce worker, stocker, and then head checker. I stayed with Buttrey for over a decade and was extremely grateful for being hired there. At that time, Buttrey was one of the better places to be hired in Lewistown. Louie turned out to be a very good boss and friend. I was very lucky to work for such a person as him. Louie once told me that a successful manager always surrounded himself with competent, hard-working, and loyal people. He expressed to me that I was at the very top of that list.

We went along with our lives as best we could. Patty eased up a little on her drama, Mary eased up some on her drinking and drug use while pregnant, and although I was getting only minimum wage at Buttrey, at least it was some money coming in. Mom started receiving chemo for her cancer and in short while her beautiful wavy black hair was gone. As her stomach grew bigger, the rest of her body became skin and bones. Each day when I looked at this shadow of what use to be my mother, it was a reality check preparing me to pull my boot straps up and steel myself for the responsibilities that would be passed on to me.

ANOTHER LIFE

I remember Mary going into labor and Gary taking her to the hospital to check her in. Then, Gary decided that he was going fishing while Mary labored! His wife was in labor with their first child and he did not have the balls to stay with her and try to give her any type of encouragement or support. Instead he was going to have yet another day of leisure and feeding his addictions. Leland had been so spot-on about this guy. When Gary made the announcement he was going fishing, I looked at Mom, with her new wig on, who silently shook her head. Mom went into the delivery room to be with Mary as she gave birth to her daughter, Jessica Lynn. It was 4:54 a.m. and my shift at Buttrey was to start at 6:00 a.m. I was very tired and I told Mom we had to get home so I could shower and get ready for work.

Mom wanted me to see the baby before leaving and I was reluctant. I told Mom I did not want to see the baby, as I did not want to get attached to yet another child, since I knew what was probably going to happen. Mom said she understood my reluctance, but that was not going to change the fact that she was my niece. So I followed Mom into the viewing area and set eyes on Jessica for the first time. Jessica's tongue seemed to be very active, and was a cause for alarm. Mom and I feared that this tongue action was a result of either the drugs or drinking Mary had done while she was carrying Jessica. We left the hospital, thankful the delivery was over, but clinging to the fear that Jessica was a drug-addicted baby.

It turned out that Jessica was in good health, and our fears were quickly dismissed by the doctor's examination. The hospital knew that Mary had both a drug and alcohol problem, so they were extremely careful to make certain that Jessica was not showing signs of her mother's addictions. As far as they could tell, Jessica was in the clear. I am sure that Family Services would have been called had it not been for Mom being there at the hospital with Mary. Mom was well-known at the hospital because of Dad's illness, and she was well-respected, so I am sure they felt that Jessica would be looked after—if not by her mother, then by her grandmother. Mary brought Jessica home, toted her around as if she were a prize she had won at the local fair, and then just as quickly took off. Again, Mom and I were the enablers. Those in families of addicts all have their functional roles. But as people will know who have been in our positions, have walked in our shoes, it was a scary path we were on. Do we watch the children so they were not put in harm's way and Family Services was not given an excuse to get involved and break up a family? Or do we put our foot down and let the chips fall where they may? There were no easy answers, and fear dictated our responses most of the time.

So Mom and I "inherited" another child. Gary was never around. He was either getting high, getting drunk, going fishing, or all three. Mary, when she was around, treated Jessica more as a possession than as a child. Did Jessica's parents love her? I truly do not think Gary did. Mary's pregnancy was unplanned, and Gary was dealing with that as best he could, pretending it hadn't happened. I do believe Mary loved Jessica with all her heart, but her penchant for alcohol, coc, and meth, coupled with an absence of parenting skills, kept her on the periphery. She was perpetually high, but certainly feeling great shame. I had always thought parenting was innate; one does not have to learn to become a parent. It is just there. I really don't know if this is true, and I am finding that I know less and less about anything as I journey further in this life. Perhaps Mary's drinking and drug use suppressed those parenting instincts. I really can't say. All I can do is speculate, and indeed these questions were running too deep for my simple mind. My mother was very ill, there was a new baby to care for, it was raining again, and soon would be pouring.

CHAPTER **15**

Right Here Waiting for You

MOM WAS AROUND for the first fifteen months of Jessica's life. She spent many hours with Jessica doing motor coordination exercises, singing and talking to her. She had read that the more interaction and stimulation given to children when very young, the better their chances that their minds would develop at a much faster rate. Overall health, both mentally and physically, would ensue. Mom was very worried that Jessica might still suffer in the future from her mother's use of drugs and alcohol, so she wanted to take any precautions she could to ensure that Jessica would have as smooth a future as possible, as the cards were already stacked against her. I believe Mom's interactions with Jessica paid off; she turned out to be a very intelligent person.

As the months went by and we saw no improvement with Mom's cancer, we stuck to life's schedule as best we could. That spring of 1989, Betty, Mom's niece, was having a hip replacement and she took it upon herself to come unannounced and make herself a houseguest and companion through almost the end of summer. By this time I had gotten a hospital bed for Mom, placing it in the living room. Betty took the couch across from Mom's bed and the "recuperation camp" was set up. Mom took much comfort in her favorite niece doing this kind and thoughtful act of love for her, and it endeared Betty in my heart for all time. Betty once again testified to the love and decency that our immediate and extended Indian family had for one another, and even though through the intolerant eyes of a stranger it looked as if we had no redeeming qualities, we always had the strongest of qualities: love.

And so that summer came, and by all accounts it was a good summer even though Mom was dying. Betty was there comforting and strengthening us, all five children were safe, I had found a good job, and we had a little money coming in. We still had food on the table. What made it remarkable was the fact that we were all together—the memories, albeit bittersweet, were being forged in our minds with the concentrated awareness that Death's scythe would soon be paying another visit to our household to claim another child of his. This time when he arrived, I promised to be there to greet him as he would gently loosen the grip that I had on my mother, not wanting to let her go with him. I knew he would ultimately win this tug-of-war, but at least this time I would be playing this game of his until the very end. I would not falter and stumble as I had done with Dad; I was much stronger this time and was more keenly aware of his deceitful trickery of trying to make me complacent. The time came when Betty had healed enough that she had to go back home and take care of matters in her household, which she had put on hold for three months to be with us. The responsibility of caring for Mom and all five children was pretty much on my shoulders.

One night, I had fallen asleep on the couch Betty had used as her bed, with my arm over Jessica's crib holding her bottle to her mouth, feeding her. I was awakened by Mom's voice for the third time that night. I got up, cranky, shaking my arm, which had fallen asleep holding Jessica's bottle. I went to Mom's bed, and she told me she needed to go to the bathroom again. I responded with a curt tone. Mom asked me to please not use that tone toward her. I justified that I was sleepy. Mom told me she knew I was tired and cranky but she did not want me to feel any guilt about this night, especially since I had done so much already. My heart softened and I grew silent. I helped Mom to the bathroom, hugged her, and then got her back to bed, where she was fine for the rest of the night. Perhaps she just didn't want to bother me again. I have always hoped that the former is true.

Mom was in stage four of the cancer and I was able to get a prescription for morphine to help her with the terrible pain she was experiencing. One of our neighbors was a registered nurse and was kind enough to show me how to administer the morphine through injections. Mom's stomach had now grown to the size of a basketball and was causing her excruciating discomfort and pain. I asked for more morphine, but her doctor refused, citing that she might get addicted. Was he kidding? Was he an idiot? She was dying—I did not care if she got addicted, and all I cared about was her not suffering with this pain when they could do something about it. First, do no harm: The Hippocratic Oath. Perhaps it should read: "First make sure my ass is covered, and then possibly do no harm."

Upon learning that the doctor would not prescribe her the morphine, she felt she needed to go to the hospital, as her time was nearing. I immediately questioned her reasoning, not that I wanted to deny her the right to enter the hospital, but because it was scaring me...it was getting too real. I started crying and shaking, thinking this was the end. Mom immediately told me to get a hold of myself, that I would never make it to the end with her if I started falling apart now. I calmed down, angry with myself that I had broken down in front of Mom, the one who was dying. I should have been the stronger of the two of us, but she always seemed to have more strength and conviction than I could ever muster. Her words brought me back to a safer place and I started to reason that perhaps, if I admitted her into the hospital, her surgeon might be able to take some of the pressure off her stomach and maybe he would give Mom the morphine she so desperately needed. Mom admitted herself into the hospital, as she did not want me responsible for any medical bills, and signing her in would have given me financial responsibility for her.

The surgeon came to Mom's room that afternoon, they briefly visited, and then I talked to him in the hallway. He explained to me that he could do nothing about the pressure because by releasing that pressure, her body would probably go into shock and she more than likely would die within a few minutes. I asked him if she could at least receive another prescription for morphine, but at a larger dose. He told me that I should be able to get that from Mom's general practitioner. I informed him that I had already tried that route and was told that Mom might get addicted. The surgeon rolled his eyes as he shook his head and told me that of course he would give Mom the prescription, further stating that if she needed more or a higher dose in the future, to contact him. I then asked him if he could estimate how much time Mom had left. He said probably no more than ten days. I wasn't ready for that answer, and it showed on my face. Mom and I had always liked this surgeon, and his actions and empathy shown me in the hallway at that moment reiterated exactly why. He wrapped his arms around my shoulders and told me he was sorry, she was a great woman. I put a smile on my face, wiped my tears from my eyes, and went into Mom's room to tell her we were going home…for the last time, I knew.

Those last nine days (the surgeon missed it by one day) were extremely hard. We still had the kids, and Jessica was with us most of the time while Gary and Mary were MIA. Patty was still drinking and having her fun and I had to keep working even though I wanted to stay home with Mom. I monitored Mom very closely each day before going to work. I would come home for lunch, give her a shot for pain if needed, and change her position in bed before going back to work and returning straight home. The kids would come home from school; I would send them to the restaurant for their supper, and then back home either to do homework or watch television before bedtime. One day while the kids were still in school and Jessica was taking a nap, Mom told me to sit down, as she wanted to talk to me. Mom told me she loved me and soon she would be gone. She expressed that she was worried about me, that I was very young and had my whole life ahead of me, and she did not want me to ruin it by taking on the responsibility of raising the kids by myself. She told me to "let go," and, although the kids would probably end up in foster homes, maybe that would not be so bad. She told me my whole life had been devoted to family and now it was time to put myself first. I smiled, my eyes watering, and was silent. I gently kissed Mom on the forehead, a tear falling where I had just kissed her, and gently whispered for her not to worry, that everything would be all right.

Mom was getting very close to passing, and the day preceding her death I took time off from work so that I could be home 24/7. That afternoon I was listening to Richards Marx's "Right Here Waiting for You," a very soft and gentle ballad. It was very popular that summer and I had played it a lot during that time. I guess Mom had been listening to it a lot too, and she asked me the name of the song. I told her. She responded that it was pretty and reassuring, and then she went into a coma.

I put the song on replay and kept it at a very soft volume, thinking it might soothe Mom in her journey. The kids came home; I explained what was happening, told them to go to the restaurant, eat, and then get back home. Patty and Mary showed up around 5:00 p.m. and did not leave as they usually did. I called Marvin and he came and stayed for a while, then left, telling me to call if something happened. I called Marilyn and told her what was happening and she said she would contact Leland and hopefully he would be able to make it before she passed. I called Betty, whose silence spoke volumes. I knew she was with me. I sat with Mom, not leaving her side once, holding her hand. Her breathing was labored and shallow, apnea becoming the norm. 10:00 p.m. came and I told the kids they needed to go to bed. Mary and Patty helped them. Around 11:00 p.m. I noticed a change with Mom, although I couldn't describe it, just sensing that something was different. I shouted upstairs telling everyone to come down. We surrounded Mom's bed just as her last breath was expelled. Having heard that hearing is the last sense one loses in death, I kept holding Mom's hand, speaking to her, telling her we loved her and not to worry about us. We would love one another and get along. I wish I could have kept that promise I made to my mother that night, but perhaps, at least in my fantasy, Dad was right there waiting for her.

CHAPTER 16

Happy Birthday Johnny

MOM PASSED AWAY on a Wednesday, and we had her funeral that following Monday, allowing time for family to arrive, and giving me a breather. Mary had been in negotiations to sell the restaurant, and that Thursday she approached me with news that the restaurant had sold and she had money for me. She handed me an envelope containing three thousand dollars. I looked at her with a tilted head, and terse brows, concise in their meaning. She told me there would be more coming, that this was a down payment to me; I hoped so, as I was owed twenty times this amount. Things were civil between my sisters and me, out of respect for our mother. I was preoccupied planning Mom's funeral. To the best of my recollection, Mary was the only family member who did not go with me to help with the planning. The night before Mom's funeral, I was there with Leland and Marilyn while we visited Mom one last time. Watching my brother and sister-in-law was very touching. Leland was holding Marilyn very tightly while Marilyn wiped the tears from her eyes. It gave me a new perspective on how I viewed my sister-in-law. Perhaps there was no war to be fought or won between us; perhaps Marilyn wasn't that hard of a nut to crack after all. Perhaps she was just like us, a softie just putting on a tough act. In many respects, Marilyn was a lot like Mom—stubborn, opinionated, and fiercely loving of children—perhaps that was why they banged heads more than once. These same traits of both Mom and Marilyn were passed down to the next generation, namely Marilyn's daughter Dorothy, a very close duplicate of her Grandma Garlick. Marilyn and Mom had many disagreements and arguments, but I knew that Marilyn was also fond of Mom. It was made evident that evening, and my heart melted for her a little that night, and it would melt further in the years to come. I imagined what memories Leland must have been conjuring up while he silently stood there. Mom had always told me that Leland was the ornery one, never silent. Mom told me that Leland grew tired of them flipping houses all the time, so Leland would try to say something negative to the prospective buyers, so the sale would not go through and they would not get another house to fix up. Mom told me that she would warn Leland to stay away when buyers came around. Listening to Mom telling this story time and time again would always make me laugh, listening to Mom refer to him as "you little shit." I wondered if Leland might be recalling the same events.

We buried Mom on that following Monday, September 18, 1989. The following day was my birthday. I did not feel like celebrating, but Mary insisted that we go to Pizza Hut "for the kids." I was too exhausted to argue. We arrived at Pizza Hut, put our order in, the food came, we ate, then I was ready to go home. The server brought over what I thought was a cake box, so I assumed Mary had ordered a cake for me. To avoid spoiling it for the kids, I sat back down to have some birthday cake. Mary had gone to the car and brought back a package, I assumed a birthday present. Again I did not want to spoil it for the kids, so I acted pleased and opened the present. There inside were Bugle Boy jeans—jeans that I had wanted for a while—and inside was a card. The card was from Mom—a note expressing her sorrow that she was not able to make it for my birthday, but she wanted me to have a good day despite her passing. My eyes began tearing…I opened the cake box and the cake was also from Mom, who had a message written in icing, "Happy Birthday Johnny, Love Mom." I guess she had given Mary the money about a week before her passing and told her what jeans to get and also to get a cake for me, signed

◀ SEEING THROUGH THE GLASS DARKLY

from her. I began crying. My birthday I would add to that list of days that I very much disdained. Yes indeed, I was a very lucky son. I still miss my mother deeply, and hope someday she will be right there waiting for me.

CHAPTER **17**

Promises Not Kept

BEFORE WE EVEN had Mom in the ground, I was accosted quite aggressively by a caseworker from The Department of Family Services. I was coming out of the post office and this caseworker was entering. The caseworker, without giving any consideration for any type of platitudes concerning my mother's death, went right for the jugular. She informed me that it would probably be impossible for me to keep raising Patty's four kids by myself now that Mom was gone. This caseworker further stated that the department would probably not be able to find a home that would take all of the kids, but was certain there would be no more than two homes involved, two children in each. This caseworker stated it would be for the best, for the children as well as me. I looked at this person with utter disdain on my face. This woman had not even given me the courtesy of mourning my mother's loss and burying her before trying to intimidate me. There had been no reports filed saying the children were in jeopardy while in my care—none that were ever presented to me anyway. Why, then, the Gestapo act? They would soon learn that I was a formidable foe; they were not dealing with a timid person, filled with fear just because they were The Department of Family Services—they would be dealing with my mother's son.

I knew that perhaps the DFS (Department of Family Services) was just trying to do their job of protecting children, which many times resulted in breaking up the home, but these children did not need protecting. They were safe with me. I would be doing the protecting...protecting them from Family Services and trying to keep this family unit as one. This struggle with Family Services would last for several years and I grew to personally hate the DFS in Lewistown. They would have their side of the story, and I would have mine. I lost many battles against the Department, but ultimately I won this war. I took this personally, and I am glad to say that my family was kept as one unit, despite their actions taken against my family.

Patty's and Mary's actions around Lewistown did not make it easy for me to protect the kids. Perhaps if I had been working at DFS, I would have been influenced by my sister's actions also. But I was not my sisters, and had proven that I was able to handle this responsibility, if they would just leave me alone so I could do this job as best I could.

Betty talked to Patty after Mom's death, and Patty promised Betty that she would not take the children away from me. The day after my birthday, I was served with papers; Patty was taking me to court to regain custody of her children, promises broken—my turn. I had promised Mom we would love another and get along. I still loved Patty, but we were not going to get along. Patty was still drinking, doing drugs, and likely dealing. I was not going to let her have custody of her children and then have to fight with DFS because she screwed up. I guess I was showing tough love? No, actually I was just tired of my sisters' shit and having to clean up their messes. I was going to look out for the kids and in turn look out for me.

I had to get busy so I contacted Mom's lawyer, who was very familiar with the family's dynamics. Bob had been over to Mom's house a few days before her passing, delivering papers that transferred the house over to Mary. The house was Mom's only real asset, and she did not want it going into probate court, so decided that Mary, with a newborn, would benefit the most by having the title turned over to her. I told Bob what Patty was trying to do. Bob was silent at his desk, thinking; he raised his head, smiled and told me he thought he had a solution. Bob told me that as executor of Mom's "estate," because

Mom had temporary custody of the children, he thought he could get that custody transferred to me as part of Mom's estate. You gotta love lawyers. This reasoning was warped but, at the same time, it was genius, treating the children as real estate. Now I knew where Neil, his son, got his brains from. I had gone to school with Neil and always admired his intelligence. I looked at Bob and replied "Really? You think that will work in court?" Bob told me we would find out.

We were in court the first part of the next week. Each side presented its case, and the judge took a quick recess to review the findings and testimony given. During the recess, I could see and feel Patty's eyes on me, glaring, burning a hole through my heart. Her anger was raw. We had been so close once, and now circumstances had gotten so bad that we now seemed to be archenemies. Her stance against me would only be reinforced at a future time by aligning herself with my sister Mary—same goals, same vindictiveness, same hatred stemming, I believe, from their substance abuse and inability to accept responsibility for their behavior. I tried to reason that it was the alcohol and the drugs behind all their actions, but soon I tired of that thinking and I gave them the gift of accepting responsibility for themselves. I tried to accept that I was doing the right thing, which I knew I was. It was hard to convince myself of this with so much irrational anger being channeled my way.

The judge came back into the courtroom, and my heart began racing. The judge did his usual regurgitation of the facts and findings and then announced that he found in favor of the defendant, John Garlick. I looked at Bob wide-eyed, not believing the judge had ruled the children were part of Mom's estate and that custody should be transferred to me, her executor. Patty's lawyer adamantly opposed the judge's ruling and the judge hastily dismissed court. Bob told me that the judge was probably on thin ice, ruling the children part of an estate, but this ruling would give us time to build a better case for me to have permanent temporary custody. This meant that I would have permanent custody of the kids, but Patty's parental rights would not be terminated.

SEEING THROUGH THE GLASS DARKLY

The following year there would be many court dates concerning the children's placement; they would all be ugly, filled with contempt—more anger than disgust, really—and it wore my emotions down. I was tired of fighting with Patty, tired of the police being called to settle disturbances, tired of dealing with the obnoxious behavior that comes from an alcoholic and drug user, tired of the manipulations and accusations. I was especially irritated that Patty was getting all the fun times with the kids (i.e. the weekends and holidays), while I had the kids on the weekdays while school was in session and there was homework to be done. Patty accused me of "going after" her children only because I had none of my own and couldn't have any of my own, her way of disparaging me as a "homo." The fact that I was a homo was not even in the most remote places of my mind. I was not given that luxury to even think about who I was as a person, least of all what my sexual orientation was. One might think that odd, but my time was so consumed by the needs and wants of others that my basic understanding of myself was on the back burner.

I had always been there for family and I guess if I had to describe who I was as a person, I would have had to say that foremost I had fallen into the category of caregiver, first with Dad, then Mom, now the children of my sisters. People have always told me that this was my decision, so basically I held my destiny in my own hands and shaped my future with those decisions I made concerning family. They were 99% right, but that last 1% counts for so much more than the other 99%. I could have said no to coming back home when Dad's health started to fail, said no to moving Mom in with me, said yes to the caseworker on those post office steps. But seriously, who could do that with a clear conscience? I would have had to have been the most self-absorbed asshole ever. Judge me if you wish, but I would hope that the majority of people would act in such a manner as I did.

During all these hard times in my life, again music was my savior. There would always be one song out there that would communicate with me; there would be a hidden message in its lyrics that only I could decipher. In its words would be a hidden strength for me to lean on and would be my friend by default when I was alone once again. At this time in my life, that song was Radney Foster's "Nobody Wins." As in the song, I wished many times that Patty and I could call a truce, but instead we kept lighting that same old fuse.

CHAPTER **18**

And So It Goes

SO LIFE LIMPED along. Mary never gave me any more of the money that she received from the sale of the restaurant, and Patty was not giving me any child support payments. She reasoned that if I wanted her kids so bad, I could figure out the money part for myself. I was receiving $300 dollars a month from Patty's ex, Gary, for all four children…$75 for each child, which was mere pennies considering his huge salary. And I was making minimum wage at Buttrey. I was in trouble financially, and something would have to give. What gave was my home ownership. I was not able to keep the payments current, so the only way out was to declare bankruptcy. I also lost my car, having given it for collateral for the refurbishing of the restaurant, and since Mary did not pay that bill when the restaurant was sold, that business took my car. I had until the first week of January to vacate my house. I found an older house in the north part of town, nine blocks away. Since I no longer had a vehicle, the move was done by having the kids help me by carrying boxes full of our possessions to the new house, a very long nine blocks in the dead of winter with the temperature well below zero. I'm not sure that being trailed by a gang of homophobic cowboys could have made it more humiliating.

 I remember one night moving boxes I got so mad that I broke down and started crying about halfway there. I started to curse Mary and Patty, all the while with the kids listening. I suddenly realized

AND SO IT GOES

they must be feeling twice as bad since one of those people I was cursing was their mother. I became ashamed of myself and stopped. I regained my composure and we continued on our way. I had asked Mary's help in moving, as she had a truck, but she was always "busy." Finally, the last night of the move, she did help and we were able to move the furniture and appliances in. The house was so much smaller than the house I had just lost, but the landlord was a saint. This landlord allowed me to purchase the house through rent payments with no interest; he paid the house taxes and paid the home insurance. He saw that I was trying to raise the children on my own and he told me this was his way of giving back to those who had helped him. He asked only that one day if I was able, to do the same for someone else. I promised I would and am very thankful to say I was able to keep that promise made to him. This Lewistown Samaritan helped me so much that I'm not sure how I would have made it without his help. I was working for $4.25 an hour at Buttrey and was not getting forty hours each week. Sometimes I was only able to get twenty-four hours, so the budget was extremely tight. There were many times while walking to work I would think that there was no way I could raise these kids by myself, make it on this tight of a budget, ever be a good role model to these kids. Then I would mentally slap myself, reassuring myself that I could do this, that I was doing this.

One Friday night after receiving the weekly pay check from Buttrey I was standing in line at the grocery store. I had gotten all the groceries I could extract from $18 that was left after paying bills, and was reviewing my belongings in my cart. I was proud of everything I had gotten from coupons and thought I had done very well to supply four people for a week on an $18 budget. I looked up from my cart and saw my sister Mary ahead of me in line. Her cart was completely loaded with cases of beer; the total would be $88 as I watched the checker ring up her purchases. I could not believe my eyes, could not believe that Mary was buying all this beer while the kids and I were having trouble putting food on our table. Then Patty came in to see why Mary was taking so long, again not noticing me. My thoughts began to race. Here were two people who could purchase $88 worth of alcohol but could not give me their share of what they owed me for their mother's funeral. Here was Mary, who could not pay me for what she owed me from the restaurant, but could purchase beer. Here were my sisters who obviously didn't care that I had lost both my house and car due to their actions, but made sure their party fun was not being missed. I went home and prepared the kids ramen noodles.

Life at Buttrey was good. I had a good boss and the employees under my supervision were very loyal and kind to me. For the most part, they respected me and helped make my job of supervising them easy. I felt very blessed to work with such good people. One Christmas I really wanted to show them that I did appreciate their contributions. So I took it upon myself to organize a Christmas party that had not been experienced so far at Buttrey. I set up a contribution fund for those who wanted to and could participate, and I also looked up any suppliers to see what they could and would donate to help make this Christmas party a success. There were drawings and first prize was an overnight stay at Yogo Inn. The party was well-attended and afterward a group of about fifteen of us decided to go dancing at Bar 19. We arrived at the bar and were having a very nice time, dancing and visiting. I was sitting around the table talking to various friends from Buttrey when this young man, who was a son of a Buttrey employee, came up to our table. It was apparent he had been drinking, and that he had a chip on his shoulder. Out of his mouth came derogatory slurs of "fucking faggot…homo…queer" and whatever else his foggy mind could spew. I was silent and just stared at the table, wondering why he felt this way after such a fun party. He suddenly lunged at me, forcing everyone at my table to stand up, as somebody blocked the punch that was meant for me.

I had remained seated. I was not scared of this kid, just perplexed about why and how he could think so little of me. I had never had a disagreement, harsh words, or bad thoughts for this kid, and yet he wanted to kick the shit out of me, because he perceived me to be different. Leaving the bar, friends followed me, as they felt this kid and his friends might try to jump me on my way home, as he had been kicked out of the bar. I got home safely and as I crawled into my bed, I smiled thinking of my friends who protected me; yes, I was a very lucky boss. I would now add Christmas to that growing list of holidays I did not like. I was holding out for this holiday, although last year Patty had passed out on the couch on Christmas Eve. I still wanted to believe this holiday could be good…I think I was wrong.

Charlee finished her last year of high school in Kalispell, having been living with a friend of mine. She told me she was not comfortable with the kids in Lewistown, and thinking back to my own experience, if there were any chance that she might be being bullied, I did not want her to have to endure that. She had enough of her own private hell in her very short life. JoJo was still in Sweetgrass, Montana going to school, staying with Betty. This had actually been decided the year before Mom passed, as Mom was having a hard time with JoJo. They certainly had not seen eye to eye on many issues and I would have to say that JoJo and Mom were very similar in personality and perhaps that was at the root of their conflicts. Anyway, Betty was having a much easier time of raising JoJo, and doing an excellent job. That left Shane and Shawn with me and for the most part, our life together was smooth sailing. I enrolled both Shane and Shawn in piano lessons, which they did not like, so I gave up on that idea. Instead, Shawn wanted to try the drums, so I bought him a drum set for Christmas and he excelled. During school recitals I would be so proud of him when he was given solos on the drums, as he truly shone. Much as piano had done for me, music came very naturally for him. I went to parent-teacher conferences, put all the kids on my insurance at Buttrey, and put the two boys in braces. Life was pretty normal except for the occasional run-in with Patty.

I was very strict with the boys, but also very fair. At one point in high school they wanted to grow their hair long and I permitted it. You would have thought I was condoning them to commit murder. Mothers were alarmed that I would allow them to do such a thing when they were teenagers. I explained to these mothers, as I had done with both boys: it is only hair, hair can be grown, and it can be cut. Until it affects their attitude, what is the big deal? I wanted the boys to learn that what is inside a person is so much more than outward appearances. I wanted them to grow up to be caring, concerned with others' welfare, putting themselves second. I guess without realizing it, I wanted them to be more like Spud than those jocks that tormented me.

One incident that happened while the two boys were in high school brings this lesson to mind. The school authorities informed me about it by telephone. It seemed that Shawn was being picked on by another boy in his class. Shawn and this boy had a history of not liking each other, and I was informed that Shane had beaten up this kid after school on school property. He received detention for his behavior, and the school wanted to make sure that I knew of this incident. I asked what had caused the incident in the first place and whether the other student had received detention. They said he had not, because Shane was the principal instigator, and they believed the other student was basically innocent of any wrongdoing. I thanked them and told them I would be talking to Shane when he arrived home, and I would be sure to handle the situation. Now I believe there are two sides to every story in most instances, and I felt that I had received only one side. I needed to hear Shane's side.

Shane arrived home, and by the look on my face had guessed the school had informed me what had happened. I sat Shane down and ask him what had happened at school today. He related pretty much what the school had said. I asked Shane why he had beat this kid up; this was not in his nature, as Shane was a gentle soul, respectful of others, and not a troublemaker. He told me that earlier in the day this student had come up behind Shawn and pushed him down the stairs. It was retribution. I asked Shane if he told the school what he had told me and he said yes. He told me the school said since there was no one to corroborate this accusation, they believed the other student was telling the truth, and therefore Shane would be the only one receiving any punishment. I was silent for a moment and then asked Shane what he thought his punishment should be. He looked down and softly said, "A week of being grounded?" I was again silent, thoughts racing in my mind what had happened today at this school. This "incident" was far more than one kid beating up another kid. I wasn't quite sure what it was; it did not seem quite like bullying, but a student was lying about the facts and the school was defending this student and giving all the punishment to my nephew. I believe that everyone has a right/wrong auto gauge inside of them, and this was just registering more on the wrong side of my internal feelings.

I asked Shane if he did not think he had been punished enough. The surprised look on his face I will always remember. I told Shane I did not like physical violence of any kind and I did not think that problems were solved with the fist. I told him to steer far from this kid, and Shawn would be told the same thing. I also told Shane I thought the school was at fault for not questioning the other student and for taking his word without question. Shane received no further punishment from me and I made a visit to the school asking why they had not questioned the other student in more detail about what he might have possibly done to Shawn. The school officials told me what they had told Shane; there was no corroboration to this story. I told the school if my nephew was hurt in the future because they did not want to dig a little deeper into this story, and that student was the cause of his hurt, the school district would be hurting financially. Two days later I received a phone call from the school telling me the other student had finally taken responsibility for pushing Shawn down the stairs and had been suspended for the remainder of the week. I thanked them, and, as I hung the phone up, a smile came to my face. This was not only for Shane and Shawn; this incident that was made "right" was a soothing salve on the wounds from my high school days.

CHAPTER **19**

The Battle for Jessica

DURING THE REARING of Patty's kids, Mary and Gary were starting to show their shortcomings in raising Jessica. Both were having a hard time controlling their substance abuse, and the domestic violence continued to escalate to a very dangerous level for anyone to be around, most of all a child. I was very much involved with Jessica's upbringing and was very concerned about her safety, to the extent that I called DFS on both of them when Jessica was about sixteen months old. My phone call resulted in Jessica's being taken from her parents and placed in foster care. This action of mine did not endear me to my sisters and made relations much tenser than they had ever been. My only concern was Jessica's safety, not about my sisters' wants, and it certainly was not because I was endeared to DFS. Per DFS's request, Mary had to enter parenting classes as well as show the ability to stay out of the bars, which she did for a few months. I thought there might actually be a possibility that Mary could indeed parent Jessica. Perhaps this incident with DFS might have scared her enough that she would realize there was the possibility that she could lose Jessica permanently.

Jessica was placed back into Mary's care and Mary did well for the first month, after which her old habits started creeping back. I tried reasoning with Mary, warning her that she was playing a very dangerous game with her daughter. I even suggested that she give me

THE BATTLE FOR JESSICA

custody of Jessica, so that she would not lose her to DFS and could still stay in Jessica's life. Gary by this time had pretty much checked out of his daughter's life, so that really wasn't an issue. Mary bizarrely interpreted this suggestion to mean that I wanted another child, and this was my first step in acquiring yet another kid for me to raise. She was totally nuts. Mary was again upset at me and I watched with sadness as my warnings became reality. Both Mary and Gary were turned in for child neglect and endangerment. I learned they had been taking Jessica to bars, having her sit there while they drank. Some unknown neighbor called DFS when they witnessed Mary dragging Jessica down the street in a stupor after the bars had closed. I was given credit for that phone call to DFS by my entire family. I am sure they thought since Johnny had done it the last time he probably did it this time. I remember Patty coming to the house and just glaring at me after Jessica was placed in foster care the second time. I asked her what was wrong, as I was not even aware that DFS was involved again. Patty told me to stop playing stupid, that the entire family knew it was me. I finally figured out what had happened through accusations and threats from Patty. I tried to tell her this was the first I had heard about any of this, to no avail. I pleaded with Mary one last time to give me custody of Jessica, but that plea fell on deaf ears. I vowed to stay out of it this time and let Mary's and Gary's actions dictate their own future with their daughter. I needed a break from this craziness; I was taking Shane and Shawn and going to Disneyland, trying to forget my family's drama for a short time.

Arriving back from California on a Friday afternoon, I was met by the specter of my yard and roof being totally destroyed by a hail storm. I was now wishing that money I had saved for two years to take the kids to Disneyland was still in my bank account. As we got out of the car and were surveying the damage, Mary drove up; I anticipated blame for the bad weather, although she began telling me that she feared DFS was going to try to terminate her and Gary's parental rights, and she wanted me to have custody of Jessica. She told me that DFS must place Jessica with me, that they did not have a choice.

SEEING THROUGH THE GLASS DARKLY

I asked her what she meant by that, and her cryptic response was to just believe what she was telling me. She stated that if she could not raise Jessica, that my taking custody was the next best thing. In my custody, Mary reasoned that she could still be involved with her daughter's life. I looked at Mary with disbelief, reminding her that she had already made it public record with DFS that she did not want me to have custody. This was also a direct reiteration of what I had expressed to her right before leaving for Disneyland—the magic of Disney. She acknowledged that she had made a mistake by fighting me the way she did, and for Jessica's sake she asked that I look past that and try to get custody of Jessica now. I told Mary I would get a hold of her caseworker first thing Monday. So much for magic. This would turn into a legal battle that would last over five years and culminate with a ruling from the Montana Supreme Court.

CHAPTER **20**

Game of Volleyball, Anyone?

THE LEGAL BATTLE that ensued over the next five years for the right to raise Jessica, I came to view as a twisted game of volleyball. At first it was a do-or-die situation. Every time a court proceeding would go in my favor, I was elated. The next proceeding might put us two steps back and I was devastated, thinking I was surely going to be defeated. Then, as time went on, and each side would give their best serve to the defense, I came to realize that I must just keep my sight on the prize, that prize of keeping Jessica safe among her blood and not having her outsourced to a foster home. At times I would get tangled up in the net of the legal jargon and lawyers flexing their muscles, and it would get scary. Then I realized that all the lawyers were just trying to do what each side had hired them to do—win. At times I became confused with the proceedings, judgments, reversals of those judgments, appeals, and injunctions. I became too familiar with the court system, and how slow justice could be. Jessica was growing up while the adults fought it out.

Having had over twelve years' experience in raising children by this time, I thought that would count for something. But since Mary had indicated to DFS that she was interested in other family members possibly getting custody of Jessica, rather than me, it set the stage for an uphill battle. Had Mary not resisted my initial attempts at gaining custody of Jessica, we would not be in this present situation. Jessica had spent the first fifteen months of her life with me and her grandmother so there was a bond there, but Jessica had been placed in a decent foster home, and she was given and shown love while in their care. I did tell DFS that Jessica would live with me, but I made it absolutely clear that Mary could see Jessica as long as she wasn't using. This, I believe, also hurt my case with DFS, and I could see their logic, but unfortunately they could not see mine as clearly. I believed they suspected that I had an agenda to conspire to raise Jessi with Mary's help. One look at our file and any person with a reptilian hindbrain would know that this was folly, that there would be no sibling co-parenting by subterfuge...but this was DFS.

With Jessica being placed back with the same foster family who cared for her the initial time, a bond started to form. The foster parents were decent and loving people, and it would be only natural for a connection to start to build. Before Mary finally decided to let go of her hatred toward me and support my desire to get custody of Jessica, I was in favor of the foster parents getting Jessica and possibly adopting her through a program called Fostadopt. I even approached the foster mother one day at the local bank and told her my feelings; she seemed both surprised and relieved. I was genuine, as my only concern was for my niece Jessica. But now that I had this chance of keeping Jessica in the family, I had to take it. I would be putting the foster parents on the defensive, never to trust my word in the future. I was not proud of this, but they had signed a contract with DFS to foster, not to adopt. I had to think of the future, what would Jessica feel when she would learn that her blood family had the opportunity to keep her in their circle and chose not to? I believed it would hurt Jessi, and I did not want that. If I failed, I at least tried. And so the battle continued and dragged on.

My relationship with Patty was getting better, and we now had a common goal of keeping Jessi in the family. We also had a common enemy: DFS. I had gone to see the caseworker that Monday as I had promised Mary, and I was met with resistance. I made my case that blood should be given preference over non-family, although my plea

GAME OF VOLLEYBALL, ANYONE?

seemed to ring hollow, primarily I believe because of Mary's actions toward DFS. Mary was usually in full combat mode with DFS. I only wished DFS would have looked at my past success in raising Patty's children and taken that into consideration when deciding Jessi's future. But I believe the caseworker was taking it much more personally than standard operating procedures would call for. In the long run the case was made much more complicated and lasted so much longer than was necessary. But I was not the one pulling the strings or playing the role of constable. DFS ruled. So all parties entered the court system where the legal ball would be tossed back and forth and ultimately the official—the judge—would decide each call along the way.

CHAPTER **21**

My Tribe to the Rescue

SITTING IN COURT that 10th day of May, 1993, I would soon understand what Mary was trying to tell me that Friday afternoon after I arrived back from California. Mary had been doing undercover drug enforcement work for the state of Montana, placing her physical safety and well-being at risk. In exchange for her work, she was led to believe that the state would allow Mary to place her daughter, Jessica, with a family member, namely me. Mary's lawyer took the position that Mary had performed her part of that agreement with the state, and she had taken an additional step of showing to the court that she meant what she said. She had relinquished her rights to Jessi to me. I also had a petition in front of the court to adopt my niece at that time.

The state took the position that yes, a meeting had taken place between officials and my sister, but no promises had been made relative to Jessica's final placement. The state would talk to DFS about that possibility, but just talk. No promises. In the end the ruling came down that there had been no contract made between my sister and the state. There had been some sort of a nebulous offer, evidently, but an offer that was not accepted by the state. Mary did actually complete undercover work, but the state did not offer her anything in return. Curious that my sister would do this undercover work out of the goodness of her heart, and put herself in possible harm's way without believing that she was going to get something out of it.

MY TRIBE TO THE RESCUE

After that court date, I felt in my heart that DFS, the guardian ad litem, and the court, all were leaning in favor of placing Jessi outside of our family. I convinced myself that placement would be with the foster parents. It was suggested that our Indian tribe get involved and claim Jessi as an Indian child so the Indian Child Welfare Act (ICWA) would apply. This meant that if Jessi was claimed as an Indian child by my tribe, the courts would have to give preference to family or tribal members, as long as the necessary parenting skills and attributes were demonstrated. In short, they would have to choose me. My tribe was notified, and for two years did not respond. What was their problem? I hate the term "Indian time," but my tribe was certainly passively refusing to be involved. The lack of response on their time zone was the polite way of saying no without having to say yes. Since my tribe would not respond, the US Bureau of Indian Affairs (BIA) was notified and asked if Jessi was indeed an Indian child. The BIA replied that Jessica was not enrolled in any tribe and her Indian blood quantity did not allow for her to be enrolled as a member of a tribe. As such, she was not an "Indian child" under the ICWA. With that response from BIA, DFS decided that preference need not be given to Jessi's native culture or blood for adoption placement.

Soon both Gary's and Mary's parental rights would be terminated. Gary's termination came first, when he did not even bother showing up for the court appearance—gone fishin'. Next, Mary's termination papers became effective August of 1993. DFS now had full custody of Jessi, along with the right and authority to grant consent to adopt to whomever they felt was the best candidate.

Again the legal ball was tossed back and forth over the court's net, too many times to keep track. With no advance warning, my tribe finally intervened and claimed Jessi as an Indian child, amending their own Children's Code of the Turtle Mountain Tribal Code to read as follows:

Indian child means a child of Indian descent who is under eighteen (18) years of age and:

(a) Is enrolled or eligible for enrollment in the Turtle Mountain Band of Chippewa Indians or other recognized Indian tribe; or

(b) Is of the first linear descent of an enrolled member of the Turtle Mountain Band of Chippewa Indians or other recognized Indian tribe.

Jessi's case just made new law because she was of the first linear descent of her mother and could now be claimed as an Indian child because of that fact.

Although my tribe was now claiming Jessi as an Indian child, the judge agreed with the BIA that the ICWA did not apply to Jessi's case, and he was of the opinion that because the tribe took so long to intervene in the case, they had no say in the matter now. In addition, this judge also gave the foster parents consent to adopt Jessi, even though DFS, who had custody of Jessi, had not given their consent for the foster parents to adopt, which was required by law. In short, the judge was circumventing the authority of DFS, which, favoring the tribe's position of the ICWA rather than the BIA's position, filed a motion in the Montana Supreme Court appealing this recent judgment. That motion, filed in early August of 1994, was denied, with the Supreme Court concluding that this case would best be served after a full evidentiary record was made. That record would take one additional year to be finalized. The caseworker for DFS handling Jessi's case still did not favor placement with me, instead favoring the foster parents. This caseworker would be removed from the case, and a new caseworker would take over. After the evidentiary record was finalized, the case would again be sent to the Montana Supreme Court. My head was spinning from the back and forth of these legal maneuverings, and I kept quiet, just trying not to get hit with the ball.

CHAPTER **22**

Drowning or Murder?

THE WEDNESDAY AFTER the July Fourth holiday in 1995, my sister Patty came to see me at Buttrey, where I was working the morning shift. She asked me if I had seen Mary in the last few days. As was typical, I had not. The last time I had seen Mary was the week before, around 10:00 p.m. when I saw Mary slapping my nephews Shane and Shawn in my yard. She was drunk and high, and I approached her deliberately and slapped her, telling her to get out of my yard and away from the two boys. Patty told me at Buttrey that she was concerned, as she had not seen Mary since Saturday, July 1st. Mary had not said anything to her about going anywhere, and had made no arrangements for her cats to be taken care of. This, I agreed, was odd, even for Mary. She adored her cats. I was not overly concerned, because Mary had disappeared before without telling anyone, but the cats, odd. I told Patty to come back at 2:00 when I got off from work, and I would go with her and try to find some information about Mary's whereabouts.

Patty returned; we, along with one of Mary's friends, started questioning people she was last seen with. The first person, a young male, said he did not want "this" to be talked about in front of his girlfriend, so he asked us to go with him to another room. We grew suspicious because we had not told him why we were there, although he seemed to already know that it involved Mary's disappearance. I proceeded

SEEING THROUGH THE GLASS DARKLY

to tell him that Mary was missing, and he indicated that he already knew. We then asked him when he had last seen Mary. During the course of our conversation with him, which lasted approximately ten minutes, he changed his story two times: first, it was Saturday when he had last seen her; then, it was Sunday...with different circumstances and explanations for each day. He was changing his story, even though it had only been a few days that had passed. Maybe it was the influence of drugs and alcohol, or something else. He then told us that the last time he saw Mary she was getting in my niece's and her husband's car. We proceeded to ask my niece and her husband if Mary had indeed been with them. They said they saw Mary at the Buttrey parking lot and had talked to her, but when they left without her, she had been with this young male we were questioning. He lied—a cold, flat lie. I was getting frightened.

We then went to question the second person, a woman, on our list. Supposedly there had been a sale of narcotics at this woman's residence that past Saturday. When we arrived at this woman's home, the young male we had questioned was already there. This woman did not deny there had been a narcotics sale at her home, and said Mary was there that Saturday night. With her next breath, however, she denied that she had anything to do with the sale, or that she had even been there that night. She also stated that the young male we had questioned was not there at the same time that Mary was. If she was not there that night, how would she know that Mary had been there or that this young male was not there the same time as Mary?

Patty then proceeded to question the young male again. He told Patty that Mary wanted the ultimate high (death) and that he gave it to her. Patty could scarcely contain herself; I had to get between her and this punk, who was smirking as he told us this. We proceeded to go to the police station and file a missing person's report. After filing the report, we went to Mary's home and noticed a trodden down path that led to Spring Creek. Mary sometimes went down to sit by the creek, but what we saw when we got near the creek frightened me and Patty. We saw a large circular area that had been beaten down, like someone had been wrestling. It was at this moment, I felt sick to my stomach, and I knew Mary wasn't alive. Patty and I hurried to the police station and asked them to start searching the creek. We told them everything; they said they would need more tangible evidence of foul play. Since they would not search, Patty and I would search for our sister. We searched for the next three days, but came up empty-handed.

I was at work that Friday, July 7, when Marsha, a dear friend of many years, came running into Buttrey. Marsha ran up to me and said she did not want to scare me, but thought I should come with her, as she had heard two men floating Spring Creek had discovered a body and they were getting ready to pull the body from the creek. I said nothing as I ran out of Buttrey with Marsha trailing me. She drove me to the scene where the county attorney, several police officers, the coroner, Patty, and a small crowd had gathered. I saw some men pulling what appeared to be a body from the creek. I tried to get closer, but was blocked by the police. I walked over to Patty and asked her if it was Mary; she replied that she thought it was, although she had not seen the body. Patty's expression was very stoic, just staring straight ahead, arms folded, very much in shock. A group of people walking by commented that they heard one of the public officials say, "Good riddance." I just stared at them, really indifferent to the hatred they were conveying to me by what they had heard. Mary was a mother, a sister, an aunt, a friend, and a human being, and yet she was being referred to as something unwanted or undesirable, much the same as garbage.

I assumed Mary's body was being taken to the local funeral home, where the forensic pathologist, at the request of the Fergus County Coroner, would transport her body to the Smith's West Mortuary in Billings, where the autopsy would be performed. With that assumption in mind, Marsha and I proceeded to go to the funeral home, where I thought I could see Mary and identify her—hoping, perhaps, that this was a big misunderstanding. We were stopped abruptly and rudely at the back door of the funeral home by the county coroner, stating we would not be allowed to see the body in the condition it was in. The coroner never disputed it was Mary, so it was final; the body was that of my sister. Marsha then drove me home, where I called my attorney to see if I could at least identify the body. My attorney called the county attorney with that request and I was turned down again, stating it was a possible crime, and I would be able to view the body after the examination of the body was completed. My attorney stated I would not touch the body, emphasizing that I just wanted to make sure it was Mary, but I was denied. Two days later it was affirmed what I already knew; it was my sister Mary who had been pulled from the creek. The examination was done on July 8 and I was able to finally view Mary's body on Sunday, July 9.

The night when I went to see Mary, the attendant and one of the coroners were concerned that I might not be able to handle viewing Mary's body. They tried talking me out of seeing Mary, stating the body was in pretty bad condition and it was quite "explicit." I needed to see my sister, and as one pulled back the sheet covering her face, another was positioned behind me, I guess to steady me if I fainted or fell from the shock of seeing her. All I saw was Mary, Kernal. Her face was a little dirty and swollen, and her hair unkempt, but it was Mary. Again I have to say that perhaps the American Indian concept of death, our attitude of the circle of life was so different than our Anglo brother's view of death, that even in our viewings of the human body, we see different versions of what is before us. These two men seemed to think I would literally fall when I actually witnessed death. I did not understand what the big deal was and still don't, I was actually perturbed by how "ugly" they made my sister's death out to be. Mary's death was a part of a circle that we all must complete, whether we want to or not, and I needed to witness her completion so that I myself would not be incomplete.

That Friday night I wrote Mary's obituary and presented it to the local paper. I knew it was Mary, so no need to wait for identification; I needed to get in touch with family before they heard the news on TV or read about it in the papers. I also requested that the local police department tape off Mary's house that Friday night, as I felt there might be possible evidence inside. I was told by the police to not tell them how to do their job. Mary's house was never taped off, and that night, the neighbors heard what they thought was someone trying to break into Mary's house. The next day we discovered a broken window on the side of the house. We could not tell if anything had been taken from the house, and we did not report it to the police. They had done nothing we had requested of them so far, so we had no reason to believe that they would do something about this incident. In the back of my mind: Had Mary's undercover work put her in harm's way, or did her life just catch up to her? Mary's death was written off as accidental, either exposure or asphyxia by drowning. I believe there was more to Mary's death than what the official report by the coroner suggested. People knew too many details concerning her death, and drugs certainly played a part in her demise. Since an investigation was never conducted, I will never know. Mary had certainly caused trouble for many people. Many people were probably of the opinion "good riddance."

I knew someone had to tell Jessi, and I wanted to be the one to tell her. I did not want the foster family telling her that her mother was gone. News like this comes from family, from blood. I knew that there would be a battle even over this simple fact that Jessi had a right to know and needed to know. There was a discussion that perhaps Jessica was too young and perhaps this might "damage" her somehow. Again, I was dealing with the Anglo concept of life and death, very foreign to Indian tribes. I had a taste of this strange reasoning when I had taken Jessi to see the movie *The Lion King* with some friends of mine. Jessi told her foster family that we had gone to see the movie, and they responded by reporting this "incident" to DFS. They complained that the movie was too violent for a young child and alleged that I had acted inappropriately and irresponsibly by taking Jessi, who was five at the time. She was now almost seven. DFS contacted me, and I needed all the impulse control I could muster to avoid confronting their ignorance and naïf Anglo views about living and dying.

It was suggested by DFS that Jessi be told that Mary had "gone somewhere." How utterly ignorant, a crowning act of epic stupidity. When would they let Mary "return" from wherever she had gone? When would Jessi be told the truth? I literally laughed at this suggestion from those in authority, and it frightened me to think these people were in charge of Jessi's well-being. Why was everyone in authority acting so fearful of death, unless in truth they were afraid? Luckily, someone in authority came to their senses and made the decision that I would be able to tell Jessi about her mother. The foster parents would bring Jessi to meet me at the City Park. At the park, the foster parents would give me no space to be with my niece alone as I was telling her about "Mom Mary's" passing. As I held Jessi in my arms, tears rolling down my face, tears rolling down Jessi's face, walking back and forth in front of this insensitive audience, Jessi would turn her head away from them each and every time we passed them. I believe a message was being given to the foster family by Jessi: "This is my birth family. These are my people and there is a boundary here that you cannot cross."

But cross that boundary, the foster family did. At the funeral, Jessi would be allowed to sit in the family room, but only if the foster parents were allowed to sit there also. Three members of my family politely went and sat in the chapel so this insensitivity could be accommodated. This insensitivity continued as they also shared their presence with us in the family car for the ride to the cemetery. They were not family, but in our sorrow of losing our sister, mother, cousin, niece, aunt, they kept slapping us in the face with their pettiness, their mistrust. Did they think we were going to abscond with Jessi at this time? I am sure this foster family thought in their own Anglo way they were doing the right thing, but were their hearts so closed to our anguish that they could not show my family some compassion, some "Christian" love, given that they were such devout churchgoers and presumably knew these attributes?

At the funeral, Marsha told a few stories about Mary and Mary's love for Jessi. Mary once had a tee shirt with the name "Caliber

Construction," the name of her construction company, printed up for Jessi to wear. Mary was relating this to Marsha with a touch of pride in her voice concerning her daughter. Marsha said she noticed tears in Mary's eyes; there was a brief moment of silence, and just as fast as the walls came down, they went back up. Mary regained her composure saying, "Time is money, got to get back to work." Marsha's also related a story about when she and Mary had been driving around looking at houses, and Mary was giving Marsha some ideas for her house. Marsha turned to Mary and told her she should go to school for designing. Mary replied, "Losers don't go to school." Mary failed many times, and had a fundamental deficit in self-confidence. But her heart was good.

Mary was willing to give Jessi to me three years ago, but we were met with resistance. Many times while I was trying to get custody of Jessi, when I had visitation with Jessi, if we ran into Mary while uptown, Mary would turn away and I would also turn Jessi's face away so she would not see her mother. Mary and I were so afraid that if Jessi saw her mom while in my care she would report this to her foster parents and they, in turn, would report this "conspiracy" between my sister and me to the DFS. How I wished now I had let Jessi see her mother... because that chance was now gone forever. During those visits, Jessi would continually ask why she could not see Mom Mary. She even asked me if I would get in trouble with the caseworker. I told her yes. She then asked me if I would get in trouble if I went by myself; I answered no, and she urged me to go, say "hello" to Mom Mary and "tell her that I love her." There is a vital amount of information to be learned by "textbook children authorities" here. Information comes not only through textbooks, but also through the heart, and my little niece was a wonderful teacher. Too few of her students were really listening.

At the close of the funeral service, Bob Seger's "Against the Wind" was played. It was one of Mary's favorites, but there were members of my family who objected to this song because of the message it was sending, and because it was not a religious song. Patty felt it appropriate, as did I. This song described Mary's tragic life perfectly and poignantly. Mary's life was out of control; she was drifting further and further away from herself and her family. She had lost her way and I don't think she really cared anymore. Patty had tried, Leland and Marilyn had tried, Marvin and Bernice had tried, and I tried, even though at the time, when most thought I didn't care, I did. Mary was breaking all the rules that she had bent, and her life was out of control. As I sat there, listening to this song, I was tearful, and my heart was heavy with this tragedy. It did not need to end this way; it should not have ended this way.

Along with Mary, there were a lot of players in her death and the guilt was not solely Mary's. In addition to her physical death, she also had died of a broken heart, losing her daughter, and losing the ability even to see her daughter without the fear that it might cost her brother's custody of her daughter also. The mother in Mary could not stand being separated from her daughter. The concept of never being able to see, touch, smell, or talk to her daughter slowly killed her. Mary once told me, "Johnny if they take Jessi from me, I have nothing left to live for." She shared that my getting custody would still hurt, serving as a reminder that she could not raise her child, but that she could see Jessi grow up and know she was in good hands. She ended, "I could live with that."

At the cemetery, Jessi was allowed by the foster parents to receive the American flag on behalf of her mother, who had served in the Army National Guard for several years. I knelt down to hold Jessi, crying as the servicemen presented her with her mother's flag. Since it was hard for me to speak in a normal tone, I whispered to Jessi, telling her to hold out her hands, explaining that the flag was a tribute to her mother for serving her country, and to always keep it near her as a remembrance of her mother's service to others. I told Jessi to take it from the servicemen and thank them. She did as I requested and I hugged her, still crying.

On the way to the family car, Jessi informed me she would not be going to the church afterwards for the reception because her foster parents did not want her to go. How controlling and unloving these foster parents were toward my family, I will never forget. I swallowed my pride one more time and begged them to let Jessi come to the reception; they allowed Jessi approximately ten minutes at the reception. I surely wanted no part of their "Christian love" if this was the way they showed that love to others.

On the other hand, there was a very touching outreach of Christian love shown to my family by the pastor and his wife of the church I was attending. Curt and his wife, Noreen, were head of the Calvary's Covenant Community Church. Upon hearing of Mary's death, they sent a message via Marsha stating they were in Seattle, but would be home very shortly and they wanted me to know they were holding me in their hearts and prayers. They had put on the reception, supplied all of the food and beverages, and officiated at the service. Patty had not come to the reception; instead, she wanted to go to the bar. Curt asked me where Patty was and I told him she was more comfortable at the Mint Bar, and I wanted to respect that as she was really hurting. Kurt and Noreen proceeded to get plates of food ready to take over to the bar. I followed them across the street, where they met with Patty and offered their condolences and the food. I will always remember their acts of kindness toward my family. They were like Jesus reincarnate. I am sure that Patty will always remember their kindness also. What a difference between what people profess, and their actions toward their brothers and sisters.

After the reception, a storm settled in the area. It was very dark, and a cold rain coated Lewistown. It was as if Nature was telling us a serious wrong had been committed toward my sister and the universe's equilibrium was fighting to cancel all the negatives that had occurred in my sister's life, so once again a stable and balanced axis might gain control of my family's life rotation. I took an umbrella and went to the graveyard to be with Mary. At her gravesite, I sat down and told her how sorry I was, that I also was at fault, and I needed to take some responsibility for her death, the emotional part of that death. I kept thinking of the last time I had seen Mary, how I had

◀ SEEING THROUGH THE GLASS DARKLY

slapped her—that was how we parted, and this memory would forever be my punishment. I promised her that I would get custody of Jessi and that I would adopt her and make sure she knew how much her mom really loved her. I would make sure that when Jessi did a certain gesture or had that unique look, or had that peculiar idiosyncrasy that reminded me of her, I would tell Jessi so she would know that her mother was still with her. I would make sure others would not condemn my sister for her failure to overcome her addiction; I still believed with all my heart that she truly loved her daughter, and no matter what those in authority said or what actions those people might take in this case, one thing would never change: Mary would always be Jessi's mother, and I knew that was extremely important to Jessi. I sat in the rain, soaked, talking to my dead sister before I went home and wrote a long letter expressing my sadness, my grief, my anger, and my disappointments concerning my sister and her case. I mailed copies to all those involved in her case. I have always said there are two sides to every story, and I wanted to make sure my side was heard very clearly. That Mary's side was heard. This was the first step in my healing process.

Approximately one month after Mary's death, I received a phone call at work from another employee at Buttrey, saying that he knew what happened to Mary. Before going to talk to this person, I purchased a mini tape recorder. I was able to get recordings from various people describing the person who had come from Washington to sell drugs here, the woman's house where the drug sale took place, and how she arranged for everyone to come and buy the drugs at her home. How two men had "dumped" Mary's body in the creek after she passed out from someone injecting her with an "8 ball" of meth (approximately 3.5 grams). How one of the men who dumped Mary's body, along with two other friends, went to the city of Great Falls shortly after this and was staying in hotels and eating steaks, and how this man was able to pay his rent after being behind in payments. It was known that Mary had approximately $1000 on her person when she was last seen, and that the money was never found. Also on this tape was a reference to this man's mother telling the woman at whose house the drugs were sold, that if the police came to question her, to cover up for her son. I gave these tapes to an attorney and to the Lewistown Police Department. The only charges filed in this case were the criminal sale of dangerous drugs, a felony. It was alleged that this person sold methamphetamine to Mary, just before her death. This person appeared before the judge and pled guilty to criminal possession of dangerous drugs. In exchange for his plea, the charge of criminal sale of dangerous drugs was dropped. The county attorney believed it would have been difficult to obtain a conviction of the offense of criminal sale of drugs. The county attorney believed the main problem with such a prosecution was the credibility of the witnesses.

Of course, I was not there when the drugs were sold, so I cannot testify to what did or did not happen. But I know what I heard on that tape I made that day: testimony by a person who was not being influenced in any manner to say anything. He volunteered this information with no agenda or secondary gain to be had. These recordings were handed over to the authorities, and that was the end of the story. There is much more to the story than my sister accidentally drowning. I believe she had help in death. She was killed and there was a massive cover-up. I hoped that one day those involved would come forward and give our family closure, especially Jessi.

I left town for approximately six weeks after these recordings were made, because the people involved were coming into Buttrey and taunting me, daring me to make the slightest move. I pulled one person over the check stand and roughed him up a bit. Buttrey did not want any further incidents, so the company graciously sent me to another store to train new employees. I was told by the police captain what might happen to me legally if they had further complaints about me from these people. I am so thankful I believe in karma. I will get my cause and effect, and surely these people will also get theirs one day.

One of the last holidays that had not been tainted by trouble, sadness, or horror, had fallen victim to our family's curse. July 4th would probably be the most horrific of all the holidays. It would now go on my list. The list was now complete and I hated all of the holidays because of what they represented in my mind.

CHAPTER **23**

Good Things Come to Those Who Weight

IT WAS THE end of May in 1995 when the attorneys dealing with Jessica's case submitted their appeals to the Montana Supreme Court once again. The full evidentiary record had now been made, so my attorney, the DFS attorney, the attorney for the Turtle Mountain Band of Chippewa Indians, and the attorney for the respondents (the foster parents) had all put forth their arguments and reasoning why and who should parent Jessi. Mary had passed that July and I was fatigued both mentally and physically. To combat any depression that I might be falling into, I was working out almost every day at the local Civic Center. I had thought about getting antidepressants, but was worried if the authorities on the case found out I was taking medication for depression, they might use this against me. I knew that doctor-patient confidentiality was supposed to exist, but I was not going to chance giving that legal concept its full weight here in Lewistown. Call me cautious, paranoid. The judge had not followed the law concerning the ICWA and my tribe's involvement, and had given the green light for adoption to a party to which the DFS had not consented. So what weight would doctor-patient confidentiality possibly be given in the courts of Lewistown?

It was a beautiful September afternoon in 1995. Lewistown was once again in the midst of a gorgeous Indian summer. I was not enjoying my favorite month, though. I felt extremely sad and defeated, and my lack of accomplishments in my life added to my depression. On top of that, I had to put on a happy face each day so people would not suspect what I was really feeling and somehow screw Jessi's life up more than it already was. I had gotten off of work at my usual time of 2:00 p.m. and had my gym attire with me so I could work out right after work. I was the only person at the Civic Center that afternoon. My mind was racing with thoughts of Mary, Patty, the kids, Jessi, work, my house. Even with all these thoughts I was still very focused on my work out because I knew it was my only way I would be able to combat my fatigue and depression. I was weight lifting, the radio was on, and I was listening to the music, escaping into the lyrics.

In the back of my mind, I heard these words: "The Montana Supreme Court unanimously rules a Lewistown judge mishandled adoption case." I listened with intensity. "This decision sends the case of Jessica Riffle back to District Court so that the Turtle Mountain Band of Chippewa can have a say in her placement." Yes! They were talking about Jessi. The ball was back in our court, and ultimately Jessi would have to be placed with me under the ICWA. I ran all the way home, where I had a message from my attorney telling me about the decision. A new judge would replace the judge who had mishandled Jessi's case. Everything was now just formalities; I had been successful in keeping Jessi in the family.

The new judge, in a memorandum, questioned why Jessi was not placed with me once Mary agreed and with DFS's blessing. He also talked of finding no statutory basis for the foster parents' petition to adopt without the consent of DFS. He called the former judge's ruling "curious at the very least." The court found that Jessi was a legally recognized "Indian child" under ICWA, was to be permanently placed with me, and granted me permission to adopt her. The DFS repeated its position in support of my petition in a hearing held December 4, 1995 by the new judge. On January 18, 1996, the certificate for Consent to Adopt was signed by the Director of the Department of Public Health and Human Services of the State of

Montana. The exchange of Jessi into my house on a permanent basis took place January 29, 1996. One phase of life's journey was over. The foster parents had surely suffered, but my family had suffered so much more. We had arrived home, but were forced to take the long way home once again.

CHAPTER **24**

I Need a Break!

IT HAD ALSO been determined by the court that the foster family would continue to have visitation rights even though legally Jessi would be my daughter, not my niece. Even though the foster parents had not been accommodating in their relationship with me to allow visitation, making me wait at the gate at the end of the road of their farm while Jessi was bought to me, the judge encouraged "door-to-door" contact. I could understand his logic and I knew that Jessi had feelings for her foster parents, so for her sake I knew this was right. I would have allowed Jessi to visit these people, would have dropped Jessi at their doorstep for these visits, but yet again I was being forced to do something by the courts even though the foster parents should have had no legal standing for any visitation rights. I felt that this new judge was not following the law, yet again. The judge made this ruling "in the child's interests." I would also be contacted by the DFS in six months for a "foster care review." Jessi was no longer in foster care—but wait, yes she was. I was providing foster care for my daughter—no wait, my niece. I was confused to say the least. It turned out that my adoption of Jessi had been stayed by the court upon a motion filed by the foster parents, filed February 16, 1996, along with a stay of removal of Jessi from Fergus County filed February 23, 1996. So now, instead of being an adoptive parent, I was a foster parent.

Would this legal interference of my family ever stop? I needed to move away from Lewistown, away from this interference in our lives. I had accepted employment in Ketchikan, Alaska and would be moving Jessi with me after February 27, 1996. This decision to move caused the stay of removal of Jessi from Fergus County. The court entered its decision on the stay of removal on February 28, 1996. The court ruled it did not believe it had the authority to prohibit such a move; however, the court did believe it had the authority to order continuing contacts between the foster parents and Jessi until this case was finally resolved through the appellate process. The Montana court would retain jurisdiction over all parties, including Jessi.

That past January of 1996, I had paid the last house payment. My house was free and clear, and the bank had approved me for a loan for a remodel. I was going to completely remodel the house for Jessi and me. All of Patty's kids were now out of school and on their own, so I did not need to consider their welfare as much as previous. At the time of my last house payment, I was feeling that things were finally looking up, and I was feeling much better about the future. Then came the stays, the appeals, and renewed DFS involvement. I decided to make a radical decision: time to move. If I stayed in Lewistown, someone would always be in my business. People could not help themselves from interfering in others' lives. It was almost like a pastime for certain people to stick their noses in others' affairs. I had enough, I needed space, and I needed my privacy. My life had been on display for years, and I wanted to go somewhere I was not known. A former boss from Buttrey offered me a position at his store in Ketchikan, Alaska and I gladly accepted. In less than two weeks I would give notice to my Buttrey employer and offer my house to my niece, accepting monthly payments from her. I had kept my promise to my previous landlord; I had returned his act of kindness toward me by doing the same for my niece—I had paid it forward.

I knew this decision was the right one for Jessi and me, but I was ambivalent and felt that I was being forced into a decision that I really did not want to make. I had worked on my house for the past five years, and it wasn't the Biltmore Estate, but it was mine now. I was in

◄ SEEING THROUGH THE GLASS DARKLY

a better financial position and could improve my quality of life. I still had legal debt, but had made arrangements to pay each attorney on a monthly basis. I had the expense of only one child now, and Mary's Social Security benefits and the adoption subsidy payments would soon be initiated. I felt that I was losing a home for the second time in my life. I was angry with those forcing me off the road to happiness. Reluctantly, I made the necessary arrangements, shipped my furniture and belongings ahead of us, and said good byes to those I would truly miss. The morning came for Jessi and me to depart. My family had gathered at my house— now my niece's—to wish us safe travels. My heart was heavy; I was losing family again, but I knew this was the only way to obtain any type of order and peace in my life and Jessi's. I drove off with tears in my eyes. I had no comforting words for Jessi, no wisdom to impart to her that this decision of mine would be right for all concerned. I had no clue if this idea of mine would work, and anxiety started to overwhelm me. I returned to my mantra of years ago: "It will get better," "It will get better."

CHAPTER **25**

What Have I Done?

ALTHOUGH IT STARTED out with sadness, Jessi and I made the best of our trip, and we had a pleasant three-day journey to our destination of Bellingham, Washington, where we would change our mode of travel to car ferry. Our first stop was Missoula, where we stayed overnight with my niece JoJo. Second stop would be Coeur d'Alene, Idaho, where we overnighted with Louie, my former boss at Buttrey, and his family. Third stop would be Seattle, where we would spend another night with friends who had moved there from Lewistown. That third day, as we approached Seattle, I remembered a trip that I had taken there after I graduated from high school to see two friends who decided to go to college in the Pacific Northwest. A smile came to my face as I remembered that trip and the fun I had while visiting them. I always liked Seattle and had daydreamed of someday living there, but that was only a dream, and I had to stay focused and get to Alaska.

The next morning, as we made our way north to Bellingham, the sky had become overcast and there was a mist in the air, typical Pacific Northwest weather. We approached the docks and found the ferry going to Ketchikan; apprehensive about this new adventure, my ambivalence was verging on regret. We drove the car onto the ferry, parked, and found a spot on the lower deck. We did not get a room, as that was extra money, and the trip would last only twenty-four hours. That night we hit a storm, and the ferry was tossed about the sea. Jessi loved it, sliding back and forth across the floor. I just wanted to get to Ketchikan so I could touch land again.

That afternoon we docked in Ketchikan. The weather was rainy and cold, the town looked dirty and uninviting, and I felt a strong sense of uneasiness now spreading to my entire being. I walked out to the deck and looked around, thinking to myself, *What have I done?* As I would soon find out, Ketchikan was the first stop for fugitives and outcasts from the lower forty-eight. We should fit right in. We were running, but from a different law—a law that we had not broken, but a law that kept interfering in our lives nonetheless. I would also learn that Ketchikan was the rain capital of North America, averaging 160 inches annually of "liquid sunshine," as the locals preferred to call it. This nearly constant rain made it even more dreary and depressing. Jessi and I got in our car and drove off to find my new store. It would be good to see Bill, my boss; he and his family would be our refuge for the next ten months.

Working at Carrs in Ketchikan was nice, and the money was excellent. My first day at the store, kids came in for their lunch break, almost all paying with fifties or hundred-dollar bills. I asked what was up with all the kids having fifty- or hundred-dollar bills in their pockets. I was told that was the norm and soon I would have those type of bills in my pocket also. I was dubious at best. But eventually I, too, was sporting the large bills. The hours and benefits were good. There was actually no place to spend the money I was making, so saving came effortlessly. Rent and food prices were high, but that would prove to prepare me for a higher cost-of-living in the future.

I found the people of Ketchikan to be very unfriendly. Most of these people were "transplants," like Jessi and me. I would have thought, since these "transplants" knew hard times, what it might feel like to be the "new kid on the block," that they would have been a little bit more compassionate and caring in their daily interactions. The people I came to love were the Native Eskimos. Being Native American, their kindness and generosity toward Jessi and me should not have been that big of a surprise, but it was. Again, my ethnicity proved to be kind and gentle. These Native Eskimos were my saving grace from an otherwise harsh and tough community. The alcoholism and suicide rates in Alaska were among the highest in the country, especially among the Native Alaskans. A good treatment for mania would be a prescription for a few days in Ketchikan, which might as well have been Native Eskimo for "World's Most Depressing Excuse for a City."

The schools in Ketchikan were surprisingly good. A lot of the oil money funneled its way back into the education system, and I felt very fortunate in that respect. Jessi's classrooms were Montessori-influenced. She excelled and her personality began to show. She was beginning to be more at ease in her new environment.

We had a small group of friends, mainly people who had come from Montana from previous Buttrey stores, with the common denominator being Bill, my former boss from the store in Lewistown. I was more relaxed in Ketchikan, not having the daily anxiety of courts, caseworkers, and lawyers from years past.

And yet, even with the pressure of life easing, I was depressed. After putting Jessi to bed each night at 9:00, I would indulge myself with the television program *Law and Order*. I enjoyed the stories behind the programming, and would pretend that, for one hour at a time; I was living in New York City and was a part of the story. It was my mini-vacation, my escape I gave myself Monday through Friday, and I looked forward to ending my day with that ritual.

It was at this time in my life that I started questioning who I was as a person, what I might want to do with my life if I had the opportunity. I was tired of being the glue that kept the family together, the family social worker and surrogate parent. And yet, these thoughts gave me feelings of guilt, of selfishness. To think of my own needs and future led to feelings that I was betraying family—Jessi. It was not her fault she had been dealt such a terrible hand of cards, and I should be the one to help her accept her hand and make the right moves. Since I was now far from Lewistown's arm, I decided to go to a doctor and

SEEING THROUGH THE GLASS DARKLY

get anti-depressants. I am sure the doctor must have thought I was a little crazy, as I kept asking him if this would be confidential, just between him and me. He assured me many times, but I kept asking, cautious to the point of paranoia. I started to take the anti-depressants and started to feel much better in about six weeks. Life was finally getting better, and my mantra was working once again in my life. Perhaps this time it would take root. My father had taught me how to water a hard frost off of a fledgling garden.

It was also at this time that I started to question my sexuality. Many people before this time had informed me who and what I was and had tried beating it out of me. But no one had ever sat down with me and had a compassionate talk with me. Who could in Lewistown? The only reaching out to me was a note handed to me by a bagger while working the closing shift at Buttrey one night, years before. The note was hand written and read that this guy knew "what" I was and, if I wanted to meet him as much as he wanted to meet me, to come to the delivery dock during my break. My skin had goose bumps from fright—this did not seem right; something was very wrong. I asked the bagger who it was who handed her this note, and she replied that she had never seen him before. Had I let my curiosity rule my decision-making, I am sure I would have been an earlier Matthew Shepard story. Wyoming did not have the monopoly on hate, and I was very careful walking home that night.

During those years of raising the kids, I did not really think about my sexuality. I knew I was extremely lonely, to the point of crying each night, just wanting someone to be with me and accept me. I knew I was attracted to men, and that I'd had those feelings since I was very young. I also knew beyond any doubt that I had never "chosen" to have sexual feelings toward men. I sought acceptance and safety, so why in the hell would I choose to be attracted to men in central Montana? I was typically depressed, but I did not have a death wish. I had watched straight men and their interactions with women, and had heard their discourse on the beauty of the female form. I had the exact same feelings as these straight men, except I found beauty in the male form. I was what I had been created to be, a human being like any other, except I was pitching for the "other team."

I have often questioned the church's stance on homosexuality. I can only give testimony relative to what I know in my heart and mind. First and foremost, I know that I have had feelings for men at a very early age in my life. I have often thought and thoroughly dissected what religious people say about homosexuality, that it is an abomination unto the Lord, that it is a perversion, that people choose this deviant lifestyle. I find it extremely hard to accept those thoughts from these people. First I find it hard that a young child could "choose" a certain lifestyle, be it straight or gay. I believe the child is born that way, through no cause of his or her own. I have been told that God does not make mistakes. If those religious people also take that stance, how can they argue that a child born gay is a mistake, or a deviant—or worse? I know those people will say the person chose that lifestyle later in life, but I know what I was feeling when I was very young. Was I so precocious that I knew about sexuality and what it meant to be straight vs. gay at that early age? Was God so uncaring and demonic that He gave me these feelings at such an early age…feelings just as strong as those feelings He gave straight men for woman? These religious people say it is a disease, perhaps a test, possibly comparing it to a test that God presented His servant Job to contend with, giving Satan permission to inflict pain, sorrow, hurt, but not death; those infected must fight their desires, must fight Satan but never curse their God.

To those people, I reply: If any of you saw a grown man giving a young child poison in a very minute quantity, sweetened by honey, but nonetheless still poison that one day would eventually destroy and kill him, how would you react? I believe every single person would be all over that man, wanting to see him punished or even maimed and killed to avenge harming the innocence of that young child. Would anybody say to the young child that what this grown man did to him was a test, that he must fight that poison that is now in his body, that he must fight Satan? The young child must not question the grown man's motives. We should not question his motives, although we may not know why he chose to poison this child. It's all part of some grand plan. But in all things this grown man works for the good of those who love him. I honestly think and believe that no person would take the side of the grown man—so why, then, should we give God a free pass? After all, God is love, and God's love had a hand in making this life and my life. So if there is a poison in this child's life, God had a hand in giving this child that poison. I can accept reasoned critiques that I am giving a skewed perspective of being gay, but I speak for a multitude when I say, "I am that child."

I believe in spirituality, which includes for me the teachings of Jesus, Buddha, and the Dalai Lama. One of my favorite passages in the Bible is from Corinthians 13. In this passage it speaks of knowing only in part, not knowing in full, like seeing through a glass darkly. I believe with my whole heart that one day we will see that homosexuality is just one facet of human love that we have not been appreciating as it was intended; that we were seeing "darkly." And then there is Leviticus 20:13: "If a man lies with a man as one lies with a woman, both of them have done what is detestable. They must be put to death; their blood will be on their own heads." Many believe the Old Testament no longer applies; the New Testament is the new covenant of the believers. The Bible is a living doctrine, and as we progress as a society, so does our capacity for understanding, and hopefully tolerance and love for one another. Love your neighbor as yourself. I believe the Bible is an instrument for understanding and we are given the keys to that understanding a little at a time. I do not believe anyone has all the answers or the whole understanding of its contents. I believe the Bible is an ever-changing instrument, and when we are fully able to comprehend its meaning, that is when we evolve to a higher understanding. Just as the majority of the believers of the Bible do not believe in stoning anymore because it is barbaric, not showing capacity for forgiveness, compassion, or mercy, I believe one day those same people will understand that love is love, no matter the sexual orientation of the person. If I am flawed, God is responsible, not I, and I will not let Him off the hook. But flawed I am not. Ignorant people do not yet understand, as they are seeing through the glass darkly. My heart is right with my maker; I am not a mistake, and I am who I am supposed to be.

It was at this time in my life that I felt something was missing in my life: companionship. How could I tell anyone this without being ridiculed or threatened? I couldn't, because I wasn't close enough to anyone in my life to fully disclose what I was feeling. I felt very isolated.

CHAPTER 26

The Worst Mistake of All

JESSI AND I had been in Ketchikan for approximately eight months when I could no longer take it. It was oppressive: the faces, the weather, the attitudes of the people of this tiny island. I had tried being nice and cordial, but it seemed that everyone was suspicious of one's intentions. Perhaps they were still running away from their own personal demons. I was tired of the smugness and the unfriendliness shown us. It was affecting my work and I did not want to put up with it any longer. I put in my notice and would train my replacement for the next two months.

    I decided to move to Seattle, as I wanted to experience living in a city, much like in my fantasies when watching *Law and Order* after putting Jessi to bed each night. I was also interested in meeting other guys, possibly dating, and possibly getting into a relationship. I was very curious, anxious, excited, fearful, and guilty all at the same time. I was afraid of what my family and friends would think, so I kept quiet. I wanted to be alone, and was becoming ambivalent about the responsibly of parenting Jessi. I loved Jessi with all my heart, but I needed to do this for myself, much like the time I moved to Jackson Hole. At that time, I had much guilt leaving Patty and the kids, but it turned out to be one of the best decisions in my life. I never regretted doing it.

    The anti-depressants had helped tremendously, but now I was suffering from loneliness, and with that loneliness came another type of depression. My self-preservation was at stake and I needed to take the necessary steps to overcome that. The greatest and hardest concern was that of providing for Jessi's needs. The only person I felt I could ask to take over this monumental task was my favorite cousin who lived in Billings, Montana. I wrote him and his wife a letter, telling them how I felt. I also expressed my shame, and my feelings of weakness for not being able to complete the course before me. I had fought so hard to keep Jessi in the family, and now I just did not have it in me to raise another child at this time. I truly felt I needed help. I hid my loneliness like a loaded firearm. It felt too dangerous and threatening, I knew that Jessi would be cared for and loved by my cousin's family, and I hoped that his wife would also be able to give Jessi her love. I trusted them and knew they would probably understand. I would await their answer.

Their answer came swiftly, and with open arms they welcomed Jessi into their family. Telling Jessi that she would be living with yet another family was monumental. I felt like scum doing this to her yet again. She would surely think that I did not love her and wanted nothing to do with her. How could I possibly get the message across to her that it had nothing to do with her, but everything to do with me? It had everything to do with my inability at this time to raise yet another child. It had everything to do with my mental health from the years of court battles to get custody of her, the fights with her mother and Patty, and the recent multiple deaths in my family. All had taken a toll on my mental and physical state. I was beaten down and it was hard trying to get back up. I take responsibility for my selfishness in this decision and, in the future, I would view it to be one of the worst mistakes of all in my life.

The time came to tell Jessi. I sat down with her and proceeded to tell her what we were going to do. Jessi listened while I talked; she asked if I could stay in Billings also, I said no—that I would be living in Seattle. She asked why she could not live with me. How could I answer that? Shame overwhelmed me. Jessi was silent, like she also was beaten and had no more life in her little body. I never asked her

SEEING THROUGH THE GLASS DARKLY

what she was feeling, as I could see it on her face, but I never gave her the courtesy of letting her tell me. I was an asshole, a selfish asshole. I would go with her to Billings, where I would stay with her and my cousin's family for a few days, to make sure she was comfortable enough before leaving for Seattle. I found out that religion would play a major role in Jessi's upbringing with my cousin and his wife. She would be educated in a church-based school, would attend church regularly, and have her chores and obligations around the house. Her upbringing would be different than I would have done it, but they were now the parents; I needed to respect that. My cousin told me that they wanted to make sure I would not change my mind in the future and request that they surrender Jessi back to me. He told me that once they started to raise a child, they would fall in love with her, and they did not want the turmoil and sorrow of losing her from their life. I promised that would never happen, but I have since learned to never say never.

The next day I said goodbye to my cousin and his family and to Jessi. Jessi and I cried. My cousin assured me that everything would be fine and would work out for everyone. I loved my cousin with my whole heart and trusted him completely. I left with heavy heart once again and made my way to Seattle, where I would discover a completely new life than I had ever known. A new world suddenly spread out before me like a crisp picnic blanket.

CHAPTER **27**

Follow the Yellow Brick Road to the Emerald City

EACH MORNING GOING into Seattle from Renton I never tired of turning the bend on Interstate 5 and seeing the city's iconic Space Needle. I was staying with a friend in Renton until I was able to find a place of my own in the city. Each morning she would drop me off on Capitol Hill on her way to work. I would spend the day looking at rentals and exploring the city. It was an exciting time for me and I felt very much at home. I was not overwhelmed by its size; in fact, I was glad it wasn't any smaller than it was. I liked the big-city feel. Seattle was small enough to be manageable, big enough that people would not know my business.

Capitol Hill, being the most densely populated residential district in Seattle, was the center of the city's gay community and counterculture, and boasted the most prominent nightclub and entertainment district in the city. It had unique stores, mainly mom–and-pop variety, on Broadway, the main thoroughfare of the Hill, from major food stores to tattoo parlors to fringe theatres. The people on Capitol Hill were diverse and unique and, most importantly, seemed to be accepting of one another. I would find a favorite hangout spot of the locals on the hill: Starbucks at Olive Way and Summit, and it became my favorite place to hang out. I fell in love with the ambience of the

SEEING THROUGH THE GLASS DARKLY

Hill and decided that was where I wanted to live. I told some people that I wanted to live on the Hill and be able to walk to work. Most of them would look at me and laugh, saying in a good-natured way, "Good luck with that." Yet, within a week I had found my apartment, on Olive Way right off of Broadway. All that was left was to find a job, which I found the next week. I would be the assistant manager of a restaurant on Broadway, approximately three blocks from my apartment. I was set in Seattle and I felt better about my life than I had in years. I kept in touch with Jessi, talking to her at least once a week. She seemed to be settling in with her new family and the initial pain we both had felt when leaving each other was diminishing. Yes, life was indeed looking good, no need for my mantra, and transformation of my life was happening. I felt an excitement and relief in my life that had been absent for many years.

My apartment was a one-bedroom in a very upscale building, and the landlord was a sweetie. She made my first apartment experience in Seattle a very charming one, extending help and friendliness my way. I had moved to Seattle the first part of February in 1997 and I was wondering why everyone I had ever talked to about Seattle faulted the city for being too rainy. The weather was absolutely gorgeous! I would find out that Seattle was having a very unusual early spring and it was strangely nice that year, as Seattle is usually cloudy almost half the year. I guess everything was falling into place for me to make my arrival to Seattle a very pleasant one. Even the weather was cooperating.

I settled into my life with much excitement, enthusiasm, and peace. There were no tribulations to endure, no lawyers to meet, no caseworkers asking questions. Every day when exiting my apartment, I would cast my eyes toward Elliot Bay; I would see the beauty of the water, the majestic Olympic Mountains, and the Needle. Every day when I would walk downtown to exercise at the World Gym, I would get a rush seeing the tall buildings and the traffic, not quite believing that I was truly living in this great beautiful city, with its diverse and educated population. I felt like Dorothy going down the

FOLLOW THE YELLOW BRICK ROAD TO THE EMERALD CITY

yellow brick road to find the Emerald City—but unlike that Emerald City, my Emerald City, Seattle, required no green-tinted eyeglasses. The brightness and glory of my Seattle required that no one had to be protected from it jeweled brilliance. Seattleites reveled in its beauty and its tolerance of individual differences. Seattle was the quintessential of being PC, being top ten of most fit cities in the US, being very techy, a place where one could get their geek on as easy as one could get their grunge on. My Emerald City was actually green, thanks to the climate. Yes I had found my Wizard in my Emerald City and had found my way home, again taking the long way. No ruby red slippers necessary.

CHAPTER **28**

Like a Kid in a Candy Store

WHEN I MOVED to Seattle I was thirty-nine years old and still a virgin. I wished I would have known they were coming out with *The 40 Year Old Virgin* movie; I would have applied for the part and perhaps taken the lead role from Steve Carell. I would have been a natural.

In all seriousness, I was in awe of how men and women had open relationships with partners of the same sex. I watched in amazement how men held hands with one another walking down Broadway without fear of getting beaten to a pulp. Lewistown seemed like another planet. In the early spring I remember eating on the outside patio of The Grill on Broadway between Thomas and Harrison. Across from me sat two young men, obviously boyfriends, who were playing footsies with one another under their table. I noticed what they were doing and it caught my attention—no, it didn't catch my attention: it engulfed it, not letting go of its grip on me. I watched them with curiosity and with envy and with intensity. It was a good thing I was wearing contacts and not glasses, as they would have been fogged up. The two men noticed my obvious attention on them and proceeded to exaggerate their actions, I guess for my benefit. Embarrassed, I made a hasty retreat out of the restaurant.

There were many examples of this love and caring between gay couples that had me in awe. One night as I was leaving Broadway Video, I saw two gay men walking down Broadway. It was raining and the two men were having a conversation. These guys were handsome, and the man on the left was holding an umbrella for the both of them. This simple act of holding the umbrella again got my attention and provided a beautiful surprise, much like the guys playing footsies at The Grill on Broadway. This scene I was witnessing was curiously sensual. Here were two men, probably in a relationship, having a conversation, and sharing an umbrella. From the perspective of dodging the rain, it was clearly a common event, although this simple portrayal of affection, of caring, of attraction between two men was so foreign to me; they held me spellbound. I knew I was the odd man out here once again, much like in Montana, but this time I did not mind being the odd man out. It was refreshing and I did not have to be afraid anymore—I was with my own, I was with "family."

I continued witnessing these portrayals of affection in the gay ghetto on Capitol Hill, and I silently wished that I could actually experience what I was seeing. One day at work, a server's boyfriend came in and he and his boyfriend were talking with some of the other employees. I came up to the group and the server told me he wanted to introduce me to his boyfriend. I instinctively froze, looking around the group, waiting for someone to jump up with rage, wanting to beat both of them up for even suggesting they were boyfriends. Nobody made a move; the server introduced me to his boyfriend, then his boyfriend left, end of story. Again, I was in awe, how was this possible? I truly was in Oz.

In my conversations with the employees at the restaurant, a club called Neighbours came up time and time again as the place to go for dancing on the Hill. It was a gay club, but the straights loved it as well. I finally got the nerve to go one night and, because I really did not know anyone very well yet, I decided to go by myself. It was a Saturday night, I had gotten home from work around 10:00, and I proceeded to shower and get ready for my first night out in Seattle. I was excited, very nervous, and did not know what to expect. It was about a ten-minute walk to the club from my apartment and entry was through an alley. It had the feel of being very underground, counterculture in nature, mysterious, all of which added even more excitement. I was self-conscious and nervous about how I looked and how I was dressed. Those years of being called "Spud" came back that night and I was extremely conscious of my face. I was hoping people would not notice my face or, if they did, I was hoping they would be kind and just give me a pass. One thing I did have in my favor was my body. I realized that all those years of working out to relieve the high stress I was under and not being able to get anti-depressants for my sadness, having to exercise to help with my depression had worked out for the good. My body was extremely muscular and defined; very low body fat and very vascular. I knew I had a nice smile, warming people up with the flash of my unusually white teeth. I had also noticed other guys who had acne scars on their face as well and I thought they looked sexy. Not your pretty boy type, but still quite handsome. Maybe I could fare just as well. There was a long line in the alley waiting to get into Neighbours. I was wishing I would have gotten there sooner, but had no idea there would be so many people waiting to get in. The line moved fast, and in about thirty minutes I was in the club.

The music was thumping, loud and danceable, the crowd very mixed, both gay and straight and it was jam-packed. There were three different stages at various heights, and the main floor for dancing. I pushed through the crowd to get to the main floor and instantly was mesmerized by the scene before my eyes. That night for the first time in my life I witnessed the same sexes dancing with their own. The ladies were dressed to impress and many of the males had taken their shirts off, again to impress. I suddenly grew very shy, frozen in my steps unable to move, very uncomfortable with myself and the image I was probably projecting to everyone. The crowd was beautiful and I felt ugly. I kept my eyes to the floor, ashamed of myself, ashamed that I actually thought I could even fit in here. My heart was racing and my face was flushed. I needed to leave to save myself from any ridicule; from any taunting that I was sure was pending. With labored breath, I moved my cement feet slowly to a corner pillar.

Here, at least I would have something to hide behind, to lean on. I grew comfortable against the pillar, and gradually leaned on it like a friend providing support. I watched the crowd from my security pillar, still amazed at what I was observing. The air was hot from all the bodies moving to the music and there was a smell of sweat in the air, testosterone so thick it made my breathing even heavier. I so wanted to experience that androgen that was flowing so freely, but still I was frozen to my pillar, providing me comfort.

I continued on watch for around twenty minutes, when I saw this guy coming my way. He was a few years younger than me, obviously Latin, with dark features, black wavy hair, dark-brown eyes, a day's worth of stubble on his face, his face flawless, masculine. He smiled as he approached, and I kept watching him. His smile grew bigger as he got closer and he said hi. I looked around to see who he was talking to and found no one. My brows contorted in a questioning manner, asking "Me?" as I pointed to myself. I must have looked like Muriel in the movie when she did the same thing, questioning her worth in *Muriel's Wedding*. He laughed and said "Yes, you." We did our introductions. His name was Alex, and he asked why I was standing by myself and not dancing. I told him it was my first time at the club and I was a little shy, but I was having a good time. With that he took my hand and motioned with his head to come with him to the dance floor. My breathing once again became labored and anxiety overwhelmed me. He apparently saw this angst in me and squeezed my hand harder and winked at me again motioning with his head toward the dance floor. I followed, anxiety still high, but wanting to take a chance on having some fun.

We started to dance; the beat was good and I loved the music. I have always loved dancing, but never had the chance to do it very often. I have great rhythm, and have always conveyed that in my dancing. I started to relax and let go of my anxiety; my feet were no longer made of cement, and instead they were part of the dance. I smiled at Alex, and he leaned into my ear and told me I had a great smile, which grew bigger. His mixture of cologne and sweat was

SEEING THROUGH THE GLASS DARKLY

intoxicating, releasing my endorphins. At one point, Alex turned me around and drew me into his torso, his arms around my midsection. I followed his lead as we did our own version of shadow dancing, his hold on my body tightening. He slipped off my shirt to complement his chiseled, bare torso.

Soon I felt his breathing on the back of my neck and heard his breath taking my smell inside of him. The sensation, liquefying me, molded my body into his arms and chest. He gently kissed my neck, his stubble gentling pricking my skin with each kiss, sending electricity throughout my body. I turned around and placed my head on his shoulder as I took his masculine scent into my being. So this was what all my straight friends were speaking of when they talked about "her smell" being so tantalizing, evoking the senses to life, except they didn't quite word it in that fashion. We continued dancing for the next two hours, breaking to get a drink of water for me, a cocktail for Alex, and to talk. I soon noticed other people watching us dance, watching as though they were mesmerized by us, and at first I was uncomfortable, but then as I relaxed with Alex I forgot about the audience.

That night I will never forget. I saw Alex off and on at the clubs for the next several months and his sensuality was explosive for me. Because he was Latino, I learned they were as passionate in most areas of life as my own native culture. Alex was the first man I ever had sex with and he was a great teacher in love, very sweet, patient, and so passionate and sensual. I learned that Latinos are among the most passionate kissers, not using just their tongue and mouth, but their whole being. We did not quite have "that" connection, but we remained friends until he moved away from Seattle years later. Alex was my first taste from the jar in the candy store, but I no longer felt like a kid. Alex helped me become a man who could be sensual, passionate, and caring in my love life as I was in all other facets of living. Alex had given me wholeness in that area of my life that I had held off for thirty-nine years to experience. Many say their first experience was not good; mine was great…thank you, Alex.

CHAPTER **29**

Do You Need Help?

I SOON LEARNED that my gay brothers were as unsure about themselves as I was about myself, if not even more so. My confidence was increasing, albeit slowly. Most guys thought that I was very confident because of my body, and few seemed to have an issue with how my face looked. I actually was told often that I was handsome, and especially sexy, although that line was always difficult for me to swallow. I felt they were trying to be nice so my feelings would not be hurt. I have to say, though, that I was learning what handsome truly was. I had the good fortune of going out with many handsome men, and I could never understand why they would want to go out with me, but my point here is that those men who were narcissistic started to actually appear less appealing to me, less desirable and sexy. Those men who were not as handsome, but had great personalities and were kind-hearted, started to appear more and more attractive. I felt like I had won the jackpot when I would get the whole package: a handsome guy with a good heart. I guess beauty is truly in the eye of the beholder. I perfected the art of picking up men who were both appealing and interesting. For me it was a game of the hunter and the hunted, and there was the art of flirting that I enjoyed very much. I was still going out dancing and would get many phone numbers from guys telling me to call them. I soon learned who the players were and avoided them, but actually called those I thought might be interesting or fun to go out with. I was new to the dating game and I was collecting a wealth of information from these dates.

The most important piece of information I was receiving from almost every guy I went out with was they thought I was very confident and they found that very exceedingly sexy. How ironic. I imagined that I was probably the guy with the least amount of self-confidence in all of Seattle, but I was learning that was not the case. I exuded confidence. When being told this, I would smile and thank them for their kind words, never letting the cat out of the bag, that what they were seeing was a façade. I was still that teenager being punched in the face with a basketball, being "fucked" by the jocks in the locker room, being called "Spud" and having my books and papers stripped from my arms. They would never know those things. I *was* the confident one, the one with a good heart on top of everything else. I was learning to put on the face of confidence even though I felt I was walking in stilettos and at any time might fall and shatter the image. I practiced every day walking in those shoes; I did not want to go back to "Spud" and all he represented.

During September of 1997, I was working out at the World Gym in the Convention Center, downtown Seattle, and thinking that I was truly happy with my life. It was my favorite month and I was truly enjoying it once again after a sabbatical that had lasted more than the usual year's rest. I was making friends, no longer had to fantasize about living vicariously through the *Law and Order* series, and now had my own New York. I was bench pressing and noticed this well-built man in the gym. He was older than me, had dark wavy black hair and dark eyebrows; he was clean-shaven and square-jawed. He appeared very confident, almost to the point of being obnoxious, but still sexy. I continued doing my bench presses, and finished with my last lift of a set when he made his way to my bench. He looked at me, leaned over and put his arm on the bar, asking me if I needed help lifting this weight before me. I smiled, returned the flirt, and told him I was fine. He asked me if I was sure. I smiled again, telling him I was sure, and he walked away, telling me if I changed my mind he would just be down on the other end of the room. I watched him walk away, a smile on my face; he was definitely good at flirting. I continued doing my bench presses and he returned. This time he informed me that he felt I was wrong, that I could probably lift more weight with him spotting me. I told him he must be lifting really heavy today.

He stopped talking, and with a puzzled look on his face asked me why I thought that. I told him he had been exercising his mouth nonstop every time he came my way. He threw back his head and this loud gut laugh bellowed from inside, heard throughout the gym. He looked at me, smiling, telling me I was "good." Over the course of a few weeks, we saw each other numerous times, would chat, and judiciously exchanged information about ourselves. He seemed very cautious about the amount of information he would give me, doling it out on a "need to know" basis, it seemed. He was Kenneth Paul Ross, forty-six years old, born in Columbus, Ohio. He had been a psychologist in Beverly Hills and had grown tired of the California pace of life, West Hollywood, and losing so many good friends to AIDS. He eventually landed in Seattle. He was of German descent and was HIV positive. He wanted his status known to me, as he was starting to like me, and if this should go further he did not want me "freaking out" as others had done before me. He watched me as he told me his status and seemed surprised when I did not react. He asked me if that bothered me and I asked him why it should. He had told me, I had the necessary information, and I knew how to deal with it. He seemed surprised and relieved. I really liked this guy and I was not going to let his positive status change my feelings. We would deal with it, and there was too much for each of us to offer one another to get hung up on a medical issue.

Ken finally invited me out on a date. He would take me to Madison Park Beach in Madison Park. I kept telling him about this "beach" I had heard about and really wanted to see, so he told me he knew where it was and would be happy to take me there. Later looking through his date book I would learn he had put me down as "beach boy" for that night. I look back, wondering if he could not remember my name.

That Thursday night came and I went to his condo on Summit and

◄ SEEING THROUGH THE GLASS DARKLY

Mercer with a bouquet of flowers. He met me at the door and pulled me inside, threw the flowers to the side and kissed me. We never made it to Madison Beach that night; in fact, we never made it down there until almost a year and a half later. Ken told me when dancing at the Timberline a few weeks later that I was Montana's loss and Seattle's gain. He made me feel wanted.

I became a regular at Ken's and he became a regular at my place. I became more involved in his life, and we were introduced to each other's friends. I started to learn about his family, little by little. My first introduction was his youngest brother, Ronnie. Ronnie was a carbon copy of Ken; same voice, mannerisms, intelligence, and very much the same sense of humor. He also was a psychologist like Ken. Ronnie and Ken were extremely close to one another—insofar as one could get "close" to Ken, as I would come to find out. Ken was thirteen when Ronnie was born, and there was a special bond between them. Ronnie had a beautiful wife, Dushka, who was one of the best mothers I have ever known. Their two girls, Miranda and Kate, were both very sweet and open-minded. Miranda was very much involved with dance and Kate was the tomboy.

Judith was his sister and, over the years, I grew closer to Judy. She was a teacher and had one son, Christian, and one daughter, Laurie. Both were mild-mannered like their mother. Randy, the second oldest brother, I knew the least. He and his family came one summer to visit Ken, and that is where I met Gail his wife. I did not know how to take Gail at first, but over the years I can truly state that I like her. With Gail, it was you get what you see. I liked that. Their two daughters, Emma and Audrey, were simply beautiful.

Ken's parents, Glenn and Barb, I would get to know at a much later date.

I would learn early in our relationship that the biggest difference between us was how we had been raised. Being from an Indian culture, there was much touching and verbal affirmation of our love for one another in my family. Even when my family would go shopping we would kiss each other goodbye and tell one another we loved the other. I would try to pass that on to Ken, only to have a wall put up when trying to show my affection toward him. My demonstrations of affection were strange to him, and his lack of affection was equally strange to me. Ken told me that his family loved one another and were very devoted in their relationships with one another, but displays of affection were rare in his family, especially among the siblings and between his parents. Was Ken telling me the truth, or was this an escape for him? I really don't know, but I accepted this as his truth and I worked with that truth as best I could.

That next February of 1998 after seeing Ken's home, I moved out of my one-bedroom apartment into a small studio of less than five hundred square feet. I was spending too much money on housing, and this would save on my rent. I had a goal of buying my own place someday, so this move would be the first step in that process. After seeing Ken's lovely condo, I was energized to do whatever was necessary to one day have my own place in Seattle. I would live in this studio for the next four years, and then I would have enough saved to put a sizeable down payment on a condominium.

My relationship with Ken was perplexing, to say the least. I believed Ken had feelings for me, but was never quite sure where his head was. I was very clear where my head was concerning my feelings for him. I loved him and wanted to be close to him. Ken was intelligent, funny, handsome, and took care of me. When I say Ken took care of me, I need to explain that he took care of my physical wants. He cooked for me, which he loved doing, he escorted me around with his car, we had companionship. The emotional part of Ken was lacking so much of the time. He would allow me to get close, and then when I would get too close, he would push me away and push hard. This was my first true romantic relationship with another human being, so I was doing on-the-job training. I would remain silent and accept anything that Ken would do in the relationship, never questioning, never getting upset, not wanting to rock the boat. I certainly did not want to lose Ken, and wanted to be patient no matter what the circumstances might be.

◀ SEEING THROUGH THE GLASS DARKLY

I remember our first Christmas together. We had spent Christmas Eve together and the better part of Christmas Day. At around 5:00, Ken announced that he was tired and not feeling well and he was sorry but I would need to go home. I was caught off guard by his announcement and had made no plans to be with anyone, as I thought I would be spending my time with Ken. I offered some words of encouragement, but I was not connecting the dots. I was hurt by this "notification to evacuate the premises." Ken hurriedly escorted me to the front door, said goodbye without a kiss, and closed the door behind me. I stood there, confused and hurt; did Ken not realize this was Christmas Day and what he had just done to me? I did not want to go home to an empty house. I did not want to be alone, so I went to Club Seattle—a bath house—and spent the remainder of my night there. This would be a repeat occurrence over the next five years, never knowing where Ken was with his emotions, just accepting what he felt like dishing out, whether that was good or bad, never questioning, never getting outwardly upset, always silent and accepting his unpredictable and emotionally callous behavior. Of course Ken was good to me also, but I always made excuses for this emotionally erratic behavior. So I was part of the problem, and I take responsibility for that. It just took me awhile to realize that my behavior was not helping our situation.

In the fall of 1999, Ken decided he wanted to go to Spain and teach English. He was having self-worth issues because of his HIV status. At the time of his diagnosis with AIDS, in 1995, Ken had asked the doctor what time frame he might be looking at. The doctor responded that he would not try reading Tolstoy's *War and Peace* if he were Ken. Ken would always laugh when he told me this story; it always made me snigger too. With that doctor's opinion, one could readily see where Ken got the impression that he was surely going to die with this disease. So with that prognosis—essentially to stick to short stories—Ken, on his physician's advice, quit his job and went on disability. He did not want to spend the remainder of what life he had left working. So by 1999, Ken doubted if he had made the right choices in almost every aspect of his life, because he had relied on this doctor's prediction. He was frustrated that he had short-changed himself with his career, with relationships, both in family and romantic encounters. Ken was chronically depressed and he was trying to deal with that depression any way he could think of—prescription medications, working out, traveling, recreational drugs, and me. I am happy Ken chose me in trying to help him out of this funk. It was therapy for the both of us.

Ken asked me if I would watch his condo for the three months that he would be gone. I was happy to do this for him, as it would get me out of the shoebox I was living in, and I loved being in Ken's condo. It would make me feel closer to him. I asked him to not wash some of his shirts before he left because I would have his scent with me and I would sleep with a shirt each night. Before Ken left, he gave me Sarah McLachlan's album, *Surfacing*. On that CD were three songs that I fell in love with: "Angel," "Full of Grace," and "I Love You." I think anyone who has heard these songs would admit that they are tear-jerkers, and to this day when I hear them I think of Ken and that period in our lives. Because of its message and because it is a reminder of Ken, I get tearful every single time I hear Sarah's voice. It is one of those very bittersweet memories, one where it really tears you up inside, but you want to be torn up because it takes you back to all those smells, sights, and sounds of that time and for those few minutes I can once again be with Ken… the power of music has no substitute.

So Ken left for Madrid, and I moved into his condo. While living there those three months, I got much more acquainted with Ken's neighbors who lived right across the hallway from Ken. All of the neighbors would become regulars at Ken's house and would grow closer to him as the years progressed. I would anxiously wait for e-mails, letters, and phone calls from Ken telling me what he was experiencing, how he was getting along, to tell me if I needed to send him anything from home. Those contacts from Ken were sometimes long in coming and I began to worry that Ken might not love me as much as I loved him.

◄ SEEING THROUGH THE GLASS DARKLY

After Ken had been in Madrid for a month, he told me that he wanted me to meet him in Barcelona, where he would be in about four weeks. He would purchase the plane ticket for me; I was thrilled, thinking Ken was missing me and wanting to see me. This would be my first trip to Europe and I was so excited. Shelly, Ken's best friend, would be going over there around the same time, so I was really looking forward to having a great time with the both of them. The time came for my trip to Barcelona and I literally stayed up that entire night before my flight. After boarding the plane, I slept almost all the way over there, having help from a few Xanax tablets. The plane touched down that morning around 10:30. I exited the plane, went through customs, and saw Ken waiting for me at the gate. I rushed toward him, so happy to see him again. We hugged and kissed, but something was off—Ken didn't seem very happy to see me. I kept silent, once again not wanting to upset him. We took the subway back to his apartment, and Ken was silent most of the way, forcing a smile every once in a while. When we got back to his apartment, I wanted to make love to him. He seemed very reluctant, but made a halfhearted attempt. Afterwards, Ken needed to get back to school and told me he could drop me off at La Rambla, a very popular tree-lined pedestrian mall. He told me to just pay attention to the connections that it was quite easy to find one's way back from La Rambla to the apartment building, or I could just meet up with him at Burger King at 5:00 p.m. I decided to meet him at Burger King. We parted at the Burger King, where he went to school around the corner and I began to explore La Rambla.

That night upon returning to the apartment, Ken told me that he no longer wanted to be my boyfriend. Point blank. He said that it just didn't feel right any longer and that was pretty much the end of the conversation. I was stunned. I could not believe that Ken had offered to pay my way here to Barcelona just to inform me he wanted to break up with me. I started to cry, and I asked him what I was doing wrong, telling him that I would try harder. Ken told me I had done nothing, that it was him, and he was just tired of being boyfriends. I told him we did not have to be boyfriends, and that being friends would satisfy me. Of course, I was lying, but I did not want to be away from Ken, and hoped this would work until we got back to the States, where we could discuss the matter more deeply. I was crying and I believed Ken was frustrated and did not want to deal with the matter any further, so he told me we would discuss it at a later time. We never did while in Europe; we just skirted the issue and we both walked on eggshells for the remainder of the trip.

Shelly arrived the next day and I was ready to go with Ken to pick Shelly up at the airport, but Ken told me he wanted to pick Shelly up alone and told me we could do something together afterward. I agreed, but with sadness and mounting concern. I did not know what was going on, but knew Ken really was not happy with me being there. Why had he invited me? Again, I remained silent, not wanting to upset Ken, as I knew he was going through a depression and I did not want to make things worse. He returned shortly with Shelly and seemed very happy that she was there. Ken once told me if Shelly was a guy, he would have married her a long time ago—for him Shelly was the perfect mate, except for the fact she was a female. This was not the way I had imagined my first trip to Europe would be. We did things together, but much of the time Shelly had her itinerary for the day and she liked doing things on her own. So while Ken was at school, Shelly would be off doing her thing and I would go to La Rambla. During the weekends, we would go sightseeing and see many of Gaudi's architectural wonders. I remember taking Ken's picture at one of the Gaudi sites, and he looked so bored and sad. I made the best of the trip and was happy when we were heading for Paris, which symbolized the two-thirds mark of the trip.

We arrived in Paris a few days before Christmas and I was remembering our first Christmas together and was thankful that at least it would not be as bad as our first. We spent Christmas Eve dining in a restaurant that had "outside seating," which had been wrapped in heavy plastic and warmed by heat lamps. Snow had just started to fall and to me it was a very romantic setting: Christmas Eve in Paris,

SEEING THROUGH THE GLASS DARKLY

France with a light snowfall—who wouldn't think it wasn't romantic? We had a pleasant night and retired early. The next week, we did the usual tourist sites and Ken still seemed upset that I was there. He would spend much of his time with Shelly and I would amuse myself exploring around the neighborhood, or riding the subway. The three weeks ended and I was glad we were going home. The tension between Ken and me made the trip memorable for reasons unexpected. Ken's problems with intimacy were leaking out.

CHAPTER **30**

The Years with Ken

MY YEARS WITH Ken were never boring, made up of extreme highs followed by extreme lows. I take responsibility for getting back in line for those repeat rides, even though I knew what the ride would entail. I was hoping that one day Ken would see that I did love him and wanted to be with him. I expressed as much to Ken early in our relationship, and he thanked me for being so honest and willing to allow myself to be vulnerable with him. But as with any relationship, ours was complicated and had its own peculiarities and idiosyncrasies.

Over the years we would take many trips in the US and Mexico, and we were very good travel mates. We also did many "circuit parties" together and it was at these circuit parties that Ken introduced me to "party drugs." Ken had used these drugs as a means of escaping for a while from his problems and his medical issues. He also just liked getting high on occasion. I had a phobia about alcohol and drugs based on my experiences with my family's misuse, and so I was of the mindset that all drugs and alcohol were bad. Ken had his own interpretation of that. He understood what I had gone through and he also understood why I felt the way I did about drugs and alcohol, but he pointed out that I had experienced only the addiction and destruction surrounding drugs, and if one was careful, one could experience euphoria with certain drugs and control one's use. I knew drug and alcohol addiction, and Ken was no addict. He didn't like alcohol. I

SEEING THROUGH THE GLASS DARKLY

trusted Ken completely, and so my experimentation began. I would say we probably had the whole alphabet when it came to drugs, be it E, G, K, X, T, and coc, and my experience was one of excitement and euphoria. But I must say that I was probably the exception to the rule. I saw many of my friends lose everything they had worked for because of these drugs or alcohol and I was very fortunate that I could be a weekend warrior then leave the stuff alone. It was purely for pleasure, and I was fortunate that I was able to keep such a clear boundary when it came to my use. I never did enjoy alcohol, starting with the taste, so it would never become an issue for me. I thank Ken for this experience, freeing my mind of that prison I had created based on my own frustrations and negative effects and problems these "poisons" had created in my life.

A weekly Sunday morning outing to Starbucks, usually the one on Olive Way and Summit, came to be one of the most anticipated moments of my week with Ken. Ken would purchase the *New York Times*, I would get the drinks and a scone or two, and we would sit down and devour the paper. We would usually be there for around two hours, discussing articles of interest, and greeting friends. Ken articulated that he loved this time starting our week, especially when we had differing views on topics and would take the time to have intimate and meaningful dialogues. He loved the art of discussion and was a good teacher. At first, I was defensive when he would not see things my way, but he pointed out that's what discussion entailed: hearing another set of beliefs and viewpoints, hopefully contrary to what we held to be true, to open up our minds and eyes that ours was not the only way of viewing the world.

One such viewpoint that Ken and I differed on was our perspectives on certain groups of people. I certainly had a prejudice against panhandlers and people who used their race or ethnicity as a means of justifying the end result they hoped to achieve. Ken would always differ with me on this. He would always say, "John Boy, you have no idea what those people have gone through, or why they act in the manner they do, you do not have their experiences; it is wrong

THE YEARS WITH KEN

to judge them." I would tell Ken he was very book smart, but when it came to street smarts, he was very lacking, and I believed many people took advantage of him because of that. He told me he was okay with that, and this was his experience in life.

One such example was a man suffering from schizophrenia who frequented Starbucks. The crew at Starbucks was always patient with those less fortunate and, even though the staff was professional, they still had big hearts. This made Seattle's Starbucks on the Hill different than most of their other outlets and, because of those qualities shown by the staff, this store was dear to my heart. The staff was always patient with this schizophrenic, and Ken was always curious about what made this gentleman tick. He would always approach Ken, asking for a cigarette, which Ken would always give him. What was unusual was that this guy never talked to anyone else except Ken, and Ken recognized this. When they had their first encounter, there was no talking between them; Ken just offered him the cigarette. As time progressed, Ken would ignore the man coming up to him and eventually the man would have to ask him for the cigarette if he wanted one. It was as if Ken was doing a study of this man in public and it fascinated him. Ken pretty much viewed the world as he did this man, and was always open to new ideas and views. Ken loved spontaneous interactions with his fellow man, and felt that change could always happen if we were open to it. But first we had to be open to change before we could expect it from another human being. It took me years to accept this "teaching" from Ken, but eventually I did, and I feel that I am a better man for it. I still have my difficulties with this, but I at least am able to entertain other viewpoints.

Although Ken was open to people of all walks of life, he still had major problems with his parents. He loved them, but never felt that he could really open up to them. Both his dad and mom had trouble with him being gay, and he knew it. Before Ken had decided on a career in psychology, he had earned a bachelor's degree in theatre from Ohio State, and a master's degree in theology. He said that his enrollment at Gordon Conwell Theological Seminary, from where he earned his master's degree, made his mother very happy. Barb was deeply religious, a "born again" evangelical. During his studies he discovered that there was too much hypocrisy in most religions of the world and he did not want to be a part of the hypocrisy, so he continued his studies switching to clinical psychology, and earned a Ph.D. from Fuller Theological Seminary in Pasadena. He ultimately set up his psychology practice in Beverly Hills. I saw Ken read the Bible many times and he told me that he felt the Bible, the Quran, the Torah, and the Tripitaka, to name a few of the holy books, were all good and had pretty much the same message. He was a voracious reader. Ken believed that if the teachings of these books were observed and practiced by their followers, and their own dogmas were not attached to the teachings, it would be a pretty simple thing to follow, obey, and believe in. Ken believed his mother never forgave him for not entering a career in theology or even divinity, a career with which he had briefly flirted.

At one point, Barb came to visit Ken in Seattle. Ken invited me to go with him, his mother, Shelly, and another friend to dinner one night. We were to go out to a seafood restaurant, as Ken told me his mother really liked oysters. Since Seattle had a great selection of fresh seafood, he wanted his mother to take advantage of that. Ken told me to order what I wanted, so I ordered fried oysters, which I really liked, but infrequently had the chance to indulge in because they were too expensive on my budget. Barbara graciously picked the tab up. The next day Ken told me that his mother thought I had taken advantage of the situation by ordering one of the most expensive items on the menu. I felt embarrassed and wanted to explain myself to his mother. Ken told me not to say anything, as his mother would get over it and it would just make things worse. I had so wanted Barbara to like me and it seemed I was off on the wrong foot. The next day, I was with Ken and Barb going somewhere in Ken's car. At one point, the subject of Indians came up and Ken mentioned that I was a registered member of a tribe. Barb made a very racist, unflattering remark about Native Americans, about the Indians, my people. I recalled my

THE YEARS WITH KEN

beautiful, loving mother and how this woman had just cut my mother down. She might as well have called my mother a bitch; it would not have hurt any more. I did not object to this "joke," remaining silent and red-faced as Ken and his mother laughed at my expense, all the time Ken looking nervously back toward me. I quietly laughed with them and excused myself from the car and walked home, hurt that Ken did not protect me from this abuse.

This was a turning point for me, and I started to find my voice with Ken. Years later I would throw this event forcibly into Ken's face, asking him how he could let his mother get away with that remark. I had never let any of my family talk bad about Ken, my love, but he must have thought it was okay for his mother to do that to me. It was very obvious this woman did not like me; in fact, it seemed she despised me. All I ever did was love her son with my whole being, but perhaps to Barb I did not measure up to Christopher, Ken's former partner, of ten years. Christopher was a very well-coiffed, worldly, and proper Englishman. Perhaps I represented the fact that Ken was a disappointment to her at some level of consciousness—he had not become a pastor as he once spoke of doing, and he was gay. At a later time, Barbara would see my love for Ken was genuine and eventually we both would heal the wounds that had been opened. I believe Barbara was fueled by a global sense of anger and disappointment with herself and her own life. I just happened to get caught in the crossfire. There seemed to be a lot of that in my life. Perhaps I was being taught something, perhaps it was karma, perhaps I just had bad luck, or perhaps I had no idea what the hell I was talking about. But it was clear that Barb did not like me.

Years later I would be opening my door to welcome my present partner's mother into our home, the same morning that Barb would say goodbye to this world and the same day that Ronnie would be celebrating his 49th birthday. A door opening, a door closing, saying hello, saying goodbye, celebrating a birth, celebrating a death, the yin and yang, the full circle of life. I truly believe there is a rhyme and reason in this life; we just usually are unaware, as if we are seeing through the glass darkly.

SEEING THROUGH THE GLASS DARKLY

In July of 2003 I received a phone call from Jessi, who asked if she could come to Seattle and live with me. Through several conversations during the next few weeks, I determined that Jessica was dissatisfied with life in Billings, because my cousin was imposing rules and regulations that most teenagers resent. I informed Jessi that no matter where she lived, whether it was with my cousin or with me, she would always have to live by the rules of that household. But the thing that bothered me the most was my suspicion that a campaign had been undertaken to drive a wedge between my Jessi and me because I was gay. This had become evident over the last year from talking to Jessi. She seemed angry with me during our conversations, sometimes denouncing gays as evil, even to the point of making me sound reprehensible. I knew that my cousin thought that homosexuality was a perversion and that the environment I was living in was dangerous and immoral. I knew that Jessi would be influenced by the family she was living with and I took that in stride. I had only hoped that I would not be demonized. I knew that one day, when Jessi was older, she could ask me those questions about homosexuality for herself, and she could decide if her uncle was perverted and immoral. I was not worried that truth would find its way into her heart; I must just be patient once again with my family. Everyone has a right to their own truth; my truth would not change to appease my family.

The well was being poisoned, I concluded, and Jessi's chance to grow up as a free-thinker was passing too quickly. I made the decision to go to Billings and bring Jessi back to Seattle to live with me. I still had legal custody of Jessi. I would not tell my cousin what I was going to do, because I suspected in all probability he would take legal action against me and cause a delay in her returning to live with me in Seattle. I would not put either myself or Jessi through another horrible legal process. I had to tell Ken what was transpiring with Jessi. As I imagined, Ken did not take the news well and asked if there were other relatives who could take over. I was hoping that Ken would rise to the situation and possibly help me in raising Jessi. Ken had always talked about possibly becoming a foster parent and helping kids in

THE YEARS WITH KEN

need; he had volunteered as a high school tutor on occasion. But, as I have learned in my life, talk is very cheap. I just wanted Ken to shut up if he could not put up. I would do this without Ken. In fact, however, I was scared to death thinking of having a teenager in my life, as it had been almost seven years without child-rearing responsibilities and a new freedom. I was confronting reluctance about letting go of that liberation. I asked a friend of mine if she would be willing to help me at least part of the time, and she accepted without reservation, but that help would last only a few months. Jessi would be with me once again, full-time.

So off to Billings my friend and I flew to get Jessi. Jessi had packed her belongings and had hid most of her possessions she wanted to take with her in my cousin's garage. I was amazed how Jessi had planned it out, without the knowledge of my cousin or any of his family. We arrived that afternoon and went to retrieve Jessi. Charlee was also waiting there to take some of Jessi's belongings back to her place in Lewistown. I had all the necessary papers stating I was Jessi's adoptive father, and everything went as planned. We were back in Seattle before dinner and I called my cousin to tell them that Jessi was with me in Seattle and she was safe. Of course my cousin informed me I had no permission to take Jessi to Seattle without their consent, and that they had legal options. I felt a sense of deep regret that I did not keep my promise to my cousin, but I did not want my niece being homophobic or being one of those Christians who claimed to live a life of love and acceptance—but only if you believe as they believed. I wanted Jessi's worldview to be a little more encompassing than that; I viewed her situation in Billings as critical, and she needed this existential rescue mission. I did not want Jessi to be bigoted and to be pitted against me and of the opinion that I was lower than dirt, and that if my mother were still alive, she would be so ashamed of me.

I told my cousin to do what he had to do, but after all those years in the court system, I knew a little about the law and I knew that I would be able to keep Jessi with me. I had not relinquished legal custody, and I felt anyone who would attempt to challenge me as

◄ SEEING THROUGH THE GLASS DARKLY

not being a fit parent would have to show something a lot more profound than the fact that I was a gay man. No legal action was ever taken, and I raised Jessi for the remainder of her teen years. I have not talked to my cousin since that day. My cousin is a good man and I respect and love him still. I imagine that he and his family underwent significant trauma secondary to losing Jessi, but she wanted out, and needed to be given a chance to explore the world in the absence of anti-gay Christian principles and brainwashing. Welcome to Seattle, Jessica.

CHAPTER **31**

Breaking Up Is So Hard to Do

IN AUGUST 2003, a month before I would be celebrating my 46th birthday, Ken and I had gone to Vancouver, BC to celebrate Gay Pride. While there I met up with Mark, a friend of mine of a few years, who lived in Vancouver. I had feelings for Mark but never acted on them because I was still trying to get Ken more seriously interested in me. Mark always reminded me of Rob Lowe, extremely handsome, so sexy, more petite than Ken, and very fashionable, especially in the shoe department.

During the Saturday night dance, Ken did not want to dance and, not surprisingly, wanted to go back to the hotel. We had just arrived and I was frustrated and disappointed that we had paid this money for admission and now he wanted to leave so soon. Ken had been visiting with friends most of the afternoon and he was tired. I had stayed in the hotel while he was out visiting, so I was rested and wanted to party. Ken told me to stay and have fun with Mark, and he would go back to the hotel. I reluctantly agreed, and was in a funk when Mark saw me. He held out his hand, which I took hold of half-heartedly, and I followed him to the dance floor. We had a great time that evening and I ended up going home with Mark. Mark and I did everything that I had wanted to do with Ken, but could not because of his depression and his ever-increasing irritability with me. That morning I went back to the hotel, as Ken was just getting up. He asked me if I had a good time. He seemed not to care about my answer, having asked more as a ritual. We made our way to see the parade and when it was about halfway done, Ken wanted to head back to Seattle. I said sure, and we drove back home.

I guess our relationship was very much in trouble and perhaps neither of us wanted to face that fact. It was much easier to pretend that everything was okay and be nice to one another. We cared for one another, but there was something definitely missing, there was no spark left. I cared more for Ken and the relationship, and certainly did not want to learn the truth that he really did not want to be with me any longer. Ken had tried breaking up with me two times in our relationship; each time I would get emotional and Ken would back down and let things be as they were. The first such episode began in Barcelona; now, we were both to blame and the pot was about to boil over. We had created a pressure cooker and had not released any of that pressure for six years. We would release that pressure on my upcoming birthday.

The week before my birthday, Ken told me he wanted to do something special for me. He had called Mark in Vancouver and had invited him down to spend the weekend with me to celebrate. What? Let me get this straight. My boyfriend, or at least that is what I thought Ken was, had invited another man to be with me on my birthday? Ken saw the puzzled look on my face and said, "Well you do like Mark, don't you?" I replied yes, but I told him that he had to admit this was rather odd. He did not see it as odd at all. I said okay, and thought Ken really did not want to be with me any longer. How could he say it any louder than this? He had invited another man to be with me on my birthday—he had invited another man to take his place.

Mark came down that Friday night and I was happy to see him. Although it was pleasant enough, I was still just confused. That Saturday, Ken was to cook my birthday dinner for Jessi, Mark, and me. We went to Ken's condo at the designated time Ken had chosen, only to be told by Ken that he was sorry but he had not cooked the meal, he had had too much going on that day. He told us to help ourselves

BREAKING UP IS SO HARD TO DO

to whatever we could find in the refrigerator. Feeling humiliated and embarrassed, we made sandwiches in silence, while Ken went to the bedroom and closed the door. Mark left on Sunday afternoon and I went over to Ken's, only to be assaulted with verbal abuse. Ken was very upset that we had not included him in our Saturday night plans. He informed me he had waited and never even got as much as a phone call. I tried to explain that Mark was not comfortable with him because of the "dinner incident." Ken would not hear any of this, and told me that I was extremely ungrateful after everything he had done to get Mark to Seattle for my birthday. Ken told me to get out—that he did not want to be anywhere near me. I left, feeling a mixture of anger and self-pity.

The next day, I went over to Ken's after I got off of work. Ken answered the door, asking me what I wanted, not offering to let me in. I asked him if we could talk for a few minutes. He reluctantly invited me in, but he told me that he had only a few minutes. I began the conversation by asking him if he still felt the same way about the weekend. He lit into me again. I told him I did not want to fight, that I was tired of fighting with him, that I just wanted to tell him that I was breaking up with him. He continued his tongue-lashing of me, when my words suddenly made their way to his consciousness. He asked me what I just said, and I told him I was breaking up with him. His next words were: "What? You are breaking up with me? You are breaking up with me? No one breaks up with me."

I now understood the depths of Ken's narcissism. Ronnie would explain to me at a later time that narcissism is rooted in a defective "sense of self," in low self-esteem. He shared with me that Ken's personality was such that he needed to denigrate people in order to prop up his own sense of inadequacy. Ronnie had been on the receiving end of that for years, too. Even with that narcissistic attitude being shown me, my tears started, and I told him that I had tried so hard for all those years to love him and to let him know that I did love him. But he would not let me love him. So I was giving him what he had wanted for years—to break up. He would now be free, he would not have me holding him down, and he could do as he wanted. I was not doing this to get even, to be hateful or vengeful. I was doing this because I was tired. He did not want me. I told him I would always love him, I was just tired of the irritability, the unpredictability, the roller coaster. I wanted to see how things might progress with Mark, who was kind, caring, even-keeled, and loving—everything I had wanted Ken to be, but was not. I told Ken I owed it to myself to be happy, and if he did not want to be happy with me, I should respect his choices and not interfere every time he had tried calling it quits with me. By hoping for change and by tolerating his behavior, I was clearly part of the problem. It was time for me to become the solution.

Ken had stopped talking, and had started crying. He could not believe what he was hearing. He told me that I did not want to break up with him, that I was just upset with him. I told him that was true, but I needed to break up with him. At this time, the old adage "You always want what you can't have" came to mind. Ken had fought me all these years and I had resisted. I no longer wanted to resist. I would no longer be available for Ken; I wanted to try and find some happiness with Mark. I left Ken's apartment, sad and tired of the emotional abuse that I had accepted all those years. I had finally found the strength to stand up to Ken.

That next year proved to be very long, as Ken and I hardly made a clean break. Ken and I had our "talks," but progress was slow as most of the time Ken would revert back to his old habits and narcissism. In the process of sorting through all the garbage and baggage we had accumulated in our relationship, I learned one important fact about Ken. No one had ever called him on his bullshit; I was the first. So, being the first, it was an extremely emotional tug of war between us. Ken was not about to let go of that "power" he had held over everyone for his entire life, and I was not about to take any more shit from him. In fairness, I would say I might have swung the pendulum further away from its equilibrium position than it needed to be. But the restoring force between Ken and me would just take a little bit longer, because both of us were resisting letting that cycle complete its course on its own.

In the aftermath of our breakup, some very important issues were resolved between Ken and me. Ken described that night after we broke up as something of a "Christmas Carol." That morning he woke up suicidal, then suddenly realized he might still have another chance to make things right. He told me that I was the best thing that had ever happened in his "pathetic" life. Then he addressed what I perceived to be at the heart of the matter: AIDS and his failure to deal with that issue effectively. He told me that people had thought he had dealt so well with having AIDS, but that was not true at all. He was terrified of dying, and by not acknowledging that fear had developed behaviors that he regretted. He most regretted not getting closer to me. He romantically imagined that as soon as we developed a deep relationship, it would be ripped away by his death, and I would be left behind. Ken said he realized now that way of thinking was "stupid"— predictable maybe, but stupid. He now wished that he had grabbed every day with me and made it count, making the best lovers imaginable. The most important point Ken wanted to make known to me was that, had he not loved me, he would have continued in the same pattern he was living. For years Ken had been in therapy to overcome those fears and to understand and work on his narcissism and its impact on his relationships, but this "Christmas Carol" had proven more therapeutic than the past years of therapy combined. I called him on his shit, real world. He felt that he could learn from that and become healthy enough to share his love with me without fear.

This revelation did not happen overnight, and it was a very painful and agonizing process. The innocent victim here was Mark. Mark was available and showing me all those loving qualities that Ken had been failing to show me. We dated; I would go to Vancouver, and Mark would come to Seattle. Long-distance relationships are hard to begin with, and what made this doubly hard was Ken pursuing me with great intensity. Ken knew he had a lot to make up for, and Mark knew he was at a disadvantage not being in Seattle. Mark knew he

SEEING THROUGH THE GLASS DARKLY

could not compete against someone who was in the same city as me, especially someone who was trying to be at his best. Jessi was also caught in the middle. She liked both Ken and Mark and was sad. Many times she would catch me crying and would tell me I needed a hug, then proceed to give me one. The one regret I have in this whole debacle is hurting Mark. It was not my intention, but nevertheless I did cause him hurt and pain. Mark and I have remained friends to this day, only because he was the bigger person, and I have enormous gratitude for his caring and love, of which I do not feel deserving.

CHAPTER **32**

Goodbye Capitol Hill, Hello Central District

THOSE YEARS FOLLOWING our break-up were hard by all accounts. Ken and I were getting back on track, and we were both trying harder to overcome our deficiencies that we had uncovered in our relationship. One hardship was finding out that Shelly had lung cancer. Shelly had always been vibrant, full of life, outgoing, smart, and, we thought, healthy. Shelly had never smoked in her life, so this disease was extremely unfair by all accounts. Shortly after Shelly was diagnosed, Ken was diagnosed with colon cancer. I was devastated. Ken had finally trusted in life enough that he thought he was going to live a healthy enough life that he could share his love without fear of dying. Both Shelly and Ken mustered the courage needed to fight. Both started a regimen of chemotherapy, and throughout they supported one another and tried to keep each other's spirits up.

Let me introduce Monkey. "Monkey," as we simply started to call him, was a cute, 12-inch stuffed animal given to Ken as a birthday present from his friend Harriet. Why she decided to give Ken a stuffed monkey as a fifty-fourth birthday gift, we had no idea. But since monkey had a tail that could be wrapped around almost anything, Ken decided to hang him on his dining room chandelier. Monkey took on a life of his own and became a frequent topic of conversation at

SEEING THROUGH THE GLASS DARKLY

Ken's. Here Monkey hung until Shelly entered the hospital for the last few months of her life. Ken wanted to give Monkey to Shelly because he was adorable, and to serve as a reminder that she was being thought of. Largely due to the terminal nature of Shelly's cancer, I really started to become familiar with Kim and Rachel, partners who lived in the Madison Valley and friends of both Shelly and Ken. Rachel and Kim were staunch supporters of both of their friends, giving support and encouragement and love. They were great friends, steadfast and loyal. Ken won this round.

Shelly was not so fortunate. Her cancer was very aggressive, and in less than a year it had claimed her life. We were all devastated. Ken had lost his best friend and he took it very hard, internalizing the devastation within, not showing much outward feeling. Again, music played an important role for me at this stage in my life. I remember being at Starbucks on the Hill a lot those days listening to the song "Torn" by Natalie Imbruglia. This song reminded me so much of Ken and what I was struggling with in our relationship. I was still unsure as to whether we were truly going to make a go of it. I truly felt torn, naked, and my faith was almost gone, but I still wanted to hold on. After we lost Shelly, I went once again to Starbucks, this time listening to the song "Here With Me" by Dido. As in the song, I did not want to move anything in my mind, lest it change my memory of Shelly. Scarier was the thought of losing Ken. I knew he had won this round, but those thoughts lingered in my mind. I could not rest until I knew he was truly with me 100%.

Ken and I started to talk about finally moving in together. We both had condominiums, two buildings down from each other, so we were frequently at each other's places, and common sense told us since we were together 99% of the time, one place would be cheaper than two. Both of us had purchased low and in 2007, the market was still very high. Both of us would come out smelling like roses in this inflated housing market. I really wanted this move and Ken told me he would do whatever I wanted if we could stay together—and this was what I truly wanted, to live with him. We started our search in

GOODBYE CAPITOL HILL, HELLO CENTRAL DISTRICT

earnest around November of 2006. In February of 2007, Kim and Rachel brought over a promotional flyer for a house they thought was adorable. It was located in the Central District, one hill over from Capitol Hill. I had wanted to stay on the Hill, but the inventory on the Hill was low and prices were high. In the Central District, these two variables were flipped on their heads. Prices were quite a bit lower, and inventory was much higher. We had made two offers on previous showings and each time we lost the bidding war. Ken, much more than I, liked the house that Kim and Rachel had found. Ken saw the charm in the house; I saw that it was old and needed work. As we continued our search, we kept coming back to this house on Pike Street, and Ken's vision for this house slowly began to penetrate my imagination, especially the outside. Ken was more about the inside; I was more about the landscaping, so we complemented each other, completing the circle.

We had put my condo on the market, and it took longer for me to sell than I had anticipated. It was on the market approximately forty-five days when it finally sold for 60% more than I had paid for it. Not bad for five years. The plan would be to move into Ken's place while we continued to search for our new home. We decided to place an offer on the house our friends had found for us. We anxiously awaited and, again, we lost in a bidding war. We were becoming disheartened, but we forged ahead. The inventory that we were interested in was growing smaller, so we expanded our search further away from Capitol Hill, which I did not want to do. About a month after we had lost this house, the owners sent a message to us through their realtor. The prospective buyers who had outbid us were bowing out of the picture, having learned the neighbors were African American. We had to laugh about this one, given that the house was in the Central District, where a high concentration of blacks called home. It seemed that racism and ignorance were alive and well in Seattle. Ken wanted to proceed with another offer, but I put on the brakes. I was upset that they had turned our offer down, an offer coming from a gay couple, and now that a bigoted buyer backed out, they were getting what they deserved. My background and experiences surrounding my mother and how she had been treated was coming into play, but my stubbornness worked to our advantage. One month later, the owners lowered the asking price by $20,000. Ken told me this was the time to take action, to which I replied that another $15,000 reduction in price would seal the deal for me. I wasn't being cheap or petty. I just knew that the house needed a lot of work. Ken agreed, we contacted our realtor, and within twenty-four hours we got a response that they had accepted our offer. We were making out well, even in this inflated market.

The next step would be to put Ken's condo on the market. At the first open house, we received an offer above the asking price; Ken just tripled his initial investment from twelve years ago. We were set, and were very fortunate in that we missed the boat of what was about to happen to millions of people who would be upside down with their home loans in a few short years. We decided to pay down this future house so that our equity would be over 80%. At last, Ken and I were getting it right. We were moving in together, our finances were great, Ken was making great headway in his therapy—and most important, he had beaten cancer. Life was good.

CHAPTER **33**

To the Platform of Deliverance

KEN AND I moved to the Central District in May of 2007. At first Ken did not like the area. He missed the people in his condo building and felt a little isolated. Unlike my condo association, which reminded me of the Gestapo, Ken had an amazing association, people who were friendly and always easygoing concerning the rules and regulations. Also, on the Hill he was closer to everything; in the District, stores were farther away, and he did not have the closeness of people in the same building. So it was very understandable that he felt a little lonely and alone.

Right before I had sold my place, Ken and I were going over to my condo to make sure it was ready for the next open house. As we got to the front door, Ken stopped me from going in and told me he had something to tell me. He paused, and turned away, crying. I froze, my heart beating fast, as I knew what he was going to say. His cancer had come back for a second time. He said he had not wanted to tell me and spoil the prospect of buying a house together. I was silent, not able to find the words for what I was experiencing. I started to cry and Ken took me into his arms and hugged me tightly. Why now? We were starting to get on the right path, still rough, but we were making headway. We both said the brave things that one should say in these circumstances; we would fight this and we would win again. But, having gone through this before with loved ones, I was fearful for

◄ SEEING THROUGH THE GLASS DARKLY

Ken and I was fearful for our future together. So as we moved to the Central District, this was playing out in our lives and thankfully the move served as a welcome distraction.

We tackled our new house with much enthusiasm. First and foremost was getting our house retrofitted for any future earthquakes. After that we replaced much of the old siding and put a fresh coat of paint on the house. One thing after another, we were sprinkling around that "fairy dust" and transforming this once tired house into a home that could be on the front cover of *House & Garden*. The transformation in the landscaping was especially noticeable and gratifying. The gentrification of the Central District was well underway, and Ken and I were a part of that process.

All while we were doing this transformation on our house, I began to notice a change in Ken—a change for the better. Ken was becoming more gentle, genuinely more loving, more caring, affectionate, and tender toward me. I believe confronting death—his first battle with cancer—was making that change. Ken had finally given in to his fear of dying from AIDS-related complications and had started living again. Now, ironically, he had to face death all over again, but this time it was a new thief trying to steal his life; this time it was cancer.

I would go with Ken as he started his second round of chemotherapy and then radiation treatments. The chemotherapy was a breeze compared to the radiation. Although they had pinpointed quite accurately where the radiation would be concentrated, it still left him with a very painful burn, like a very serious sunburn, with the effects lasting much longer. No matter what they say about radiation being necessary for survival, I would now question whether the pros outweigh the cons. The radiation left much of the surrounding tissues permanently scarred, unable to heal, compromising his whole system, weakening his immune system to fight off infections and recurring cancers. This round of treatments lasted for approximately three months and, once again, he was given a clean record concerning his cancer. Once again it looked like Ken had beaten the cancer. We would continue with our life, fixing the house to our liking, and simply just enjoying

TO THE PLATFORM OF DELIVERANCE

our time together. Ken and I were truly happy at this stage. We had talked about "happiness," and previous to this time Ken had always referred to being "content." Now that we were living together, he told me that he was actually happy, just not content anymore. Feeling positive and more energized about our relationship than we had for a long time, we decided to become registered domestic partners. Since marriage was not legal in the state of Washington, this was the next best thing.

After Shelly passed, we took Monkey back home with us and it was at this time that Ken started to express his feelings through this lovable stuffed animal. Ken was fearful of dying and once again wanted to make people think he was dealing with that issue successfully. Ken had always dealt with serious issues by making jokes, poking fun at them, and using sarcasm. Hardly ever did Ken deal with serious issues through somber discourse. Monkey was the perfect vessel into which Ken could place all the fears, insecurities, questions, sadness, and frustrations. To some degree, Monkey took part of those same insecurities away from me also. Monkey became an entity unto himself, equipped with a personality, likes and dislikes, and most importantly, emotions. We projected our emotions onto Monkey at times when feelings were especially hard for us to express. Ken had his "Monkey voice" and I had mine. Monkey became our collective voice and our go-between.

Those few years that we had between the cancers were amazing. Friday and Sunday nights were my favorite with Ken. I enjoyed Fridays because the work week was over and we were starting the weekend, and Sundays I enjoyed because they were very peaceful to me. I remember many Sunday evenings being on the back porch with Ken. He would be enjoying a cigarette, while I enjoyed a Coke. Ken would look at me and smile, take me in his arms, and give me a kiss, saying he loved me. He would always use the nickname of John Boy, Cutie, or Johnny and my heart would melt. This time had been long in coming and it was worth the wait. We joked about growing old, being in rockers on the front porch, trying to whistle at young men as they walked by our home. All the while, we would not be able to get the whistle out because we had lost all of our teeth. We would laugh and enjoy the moment and be thankful that we had given each other another chance to get it right.

In early 2008, Ken began to notice blood in his urine and stools. I went with him to his next doctor appointment; they did the usual tests and drew blood. Within a week we had the news that his cancer had returned for a third time. This time they could do chemotherapy, but they could not do radiation a second time. They discovered the radiation treatments they had done prior had damaged much of the surrounding tissue including part of his large intestine. The best alternative would be to do a colostomy. If he wanted to live, this would be Ken's only choice, it would "probably" take care of the cancer this time and since he was starting to have blockage issues, this operation would also solve that. Two birds with one stone, very economical. The flavor of the week this time was colostomy; it seemed to me that the medical profession really did not know what they were doing. Maybe they really didn't know that much about cancer and were stabbing in the dark. I really don't know, but my anger was telling me that I could guess as well as the team of physicians treating Ken. I was angry that they had not more pointedly warned us about the possible effects of the radiation, and now because of those treatments we were facing another new problem. I was the angry one. Ken was the kind and affable patient.

Ken had been brought up to the platform of surrendering control over his life three times now, and still he was kind. Deliverance through his cancer would be the only form of liberation from the fears of dying that had tortured Ken for all these years. This form of deliverance would be a bitter pill to swallow as both Ken and I choked upon it being administered to the both of us. I would learn much from the love of my life during his last year.

CHAPTER 34

Close the Beacons of Your Mind, Clear Your Love, Cut the Cord

THE IMPORTANCE OF music in my life had never been more apparent than it was during Ken's last year. Friday would come and it would be the end of my work week at the Rhododendron Restaurant. The restaurant was located on First Hill—or as the locals called it, "Pill Hill," because of the many hospitals. Rhododendron Restaurant was actually owned by Virginia Mason Hospital, so although I was a waiter, my employer was actually a hospital. I worked for Virginia Mason for fourteen years; they were an excellent employer, and the restaurant served excellent food. Most everyone that I worked with at the restaurant knew Ken and liked him. I would share the daily drama going on at the restaurant each night when I got home and I would update Ken on the most recent episode of "As the Rhody Turns." During those years, I developed some very close friendships with Faith, Andy, Theresa, Gogul, Elfie, and Terri, to name just a few. It was at the restaurant that I met many people who were going through life and death situations, much the same as Ken and I. It always seemed that those people who were having the roughest time were the kindest, the most patient, the most loving. Against hospital standards and protocol, when I got to know customers who were having medical issues and just generally a rough time, I would refer to them as "dear," "sweetie," or perhaps even "honey." They were

SEEING THROUGH THE GLASS DARKLY

more than restaurant customers, and some became close friends. There were several of us working there, who through many deaths of customers had become part of our "family." Some days could be very sad. Part of my support group came from these people whom I worked with, and also from those whom I served. They served me as well.

The end of the work week was rewarded with a massage most Friday afternoons. One Friday when driving home post-massage, I was listening to the radio and the group The Killers was singing "Human," a chart-topping song at the time. The voice was that of Brandon Flowers. His voice was very smooth and edgy at the same time—bittersweet. His voice just did it for me and, as I got to know his music more, his unique sound always put me in that good spot in my mind. As I was listening to the song, I was thinking about Ken, worrying what was going to happen next, and I had this very "bitter sweetness" in my thoughts, and this song amplified that feeling. I started listening to the lyrics more carefully. It was as if this song was addressing everything Ken and I were going through with his cancers. I mean, every lyric had a message for me.

When Ken first found out he had colon cancer, he did not want to tell anyone, as he did not want to upset me or his family. He was always so kind to the doctors, nurses, everyone. He would always ask how they were doing, even when he was in great pain. That autumn Ken and I were walking in the garden when he told me he was so tired of going through one door, only to have another open up. This message was very clear in verse two of "Human."

During that same walk, Ken asked me why I was still around, when all I would get was heartache. He told me to be of good heart, I had stood by him— now walk away. In verses three and four the lyrics are about grace, virtue, good, soul, and romance. These verses reminded me of Ken saying goodbye to everyone with sarcasm, trying to make light of the situation, with a twinge of resentment. When the lyrics turn to "devotion" in verse four, I would hope I could wear that title. I did not teach Ken about devotion, but rather, we discovered together a great and wonderful love. The song felt like a cautionary tale,

CLOSE THE BEACONS OF YOUR MIND, CLEAR YOUR LOVE, CUT THE CORD

as if it had been written to tell me I should prepare for Ken's goodbye, because soon I would have to let him go.

Ken and I had many discussions about whether a person should be held responsible for their actions, or should we look at the situation more compassionately and take into consideration the context, his or her background, and what might have been experienced in one's life. He asked me more than once, "John Boy, are we just mere mortals or are we something more than that? I would hope we are something more." Hence, when I hear the question in the song "Are we human or are we dancer?" it reminds me of Ken. Replace the word "human" with "mortals," and "dancer" with "something more than that."

The chorus in "Human" includes lines about his sign being vital and his hands being cold. Again, I believe this speaks of Ken all over. His body was failing him, but not his attitude and the way he dealt with life. Lastly, Ken looked everywhere for an answer. We made plans to go to New York and the Mayo Clinic. We looked into acupuncture, herbal teas, HGH, anything that would help him stay alive.

This song was on the radio constantly when Ken was in and out of the hospital during his end months. I would hear it driving to and from the hospital; it started speaking to me and I started to really listen to the lyrics and this is my interpretation. Very bittersweet, but this was our life at the end.

There are quite a few interpretations of this song's lyrics on the internet. There is even one about a man dying of cancer. Another "God Hit," as one friend of mine describes these coincidences. I hope one day that Brandon Flowers will come to know how he helped me through this time in my life by recording this song. Every time I hear Brandon's voice on the radio, I have to stop whatever I'm doing if possible, and just take his unique sound in and let his voice take me back to our home on Pike Street. His smooth tenor voice actually lets me relive those feelings, sights, sounds, and smells of Ken and our life at that troublesome and yet so rewarding time in both of our lives. His song still gives me a tear, then a smile. What an amazing gift to give to another human being.

CHAPTER **35**

So Long to Our Love

AFTER KEN HAD the operation for the colostomy, it was hard to keep up the appearance that everything was going to be okay. This operation was a major blow to Ken. He had always been so muscular, healthy, and able to conquer anything. Now, little by little, his body was betraying him, and the trust that he had put in the medical doctors was faltering. Rachel and Kim had gone to Italy for a year's sabbatical, our friend Shelly was gone, many of his friends had died of AIDS, and now he was facing these medical issues. Dealing with the colostomy was very much of a learning curve for both of us. Although his support group of therapists, nurses, and doctors tried to make it seem that people who had colostomies lead very normal lives, they did not relate the bad to us; we learned that on our own… sometimes with embarrassment, or surprise mixed with horror, but most of the time just plain frustration. Ken tried to get on a schedule to help him regulate the bowel movements, but it seemed not to help. When we thought we had it down, we would be met with surprise. So we dealt with it by having the philosophy "always be prepared." With that in mind we kept extra supplies in the car, the gym bag, and even in our pockets when we would go out on those rare occasions. For Ken, he tried to take it in stride, but I could tell he was getting more and more discouraged.

Ken was in and out of the hospital on a regular basis; soon, he was in the hospital more than he was out. During one such stay in the hospital, his mother and sister came out from Columbus. Their trip was prompted by a tearful phone call from me informing them Ken that was going into emergency surgery and the prognosis was very bleak. Previously I had gotten a phone call at work telling me I should come to the hospital as soon as I could get there. I ran the six blocks over there to find them prepping Ken for surgery. He smiled as I came through the door and told me he did not know if he was going to make it through this surgery. He did not think I would make it over before they took him into the operating room and was so happy I had. He proceeded to tell me that I was the best partner he could have ever hoped for and he would do it all over with me again if he had the chance. Then they took him away for surgery. That confession of love by Ken threw me up against the wall. I decided to break the secrecy that Ken was having with his family, as they needed to know the truth. Ken had been secretive and minimizing of his health problems, so the phone call was made, and the next day Barb and Judy were in Seattle. I had also informed Kim and Rachel what was going on, and Rachel decided to also come to Seattle from Italy and help in any way she could.

Ironically, I was a little upset with Rachel's decision to come back to Seattle. I was upset because I thought Ken might think we were all gathering for his death, and I did not want that to cross his mind. Ken surprised me with his reaction and was actually very happy that everyone was there. He told me I had done the right thing in contacting everyone. It was good to have others around for support and to talk to them about Ken. Rachel was Rachel, God bless her: very proactive, taking any initiative that she thought was appropriate and taking some of the burdens off of my shoulders. To her, Ken was the brother she never had. Barb and Judy were very emotional, as I knew they would be, but their visit was good for Ken, and he enjoyed having them around. Ken recovered from this surgery and was allowed to go home from where the five of us celebrated my fifty-first birthday. Judy and I went to the International District to the Honey Court Restaurant and picked up my favorite food, Chinese. Ken had to retire early that night, but I had had a great birthday. Ken was still with me.

After that scare, we returned to normal life—as normal as we could get, at least. Those autumn days were scary for me, because I knew what was coming and I did not want to go down that path yet one more time, as this would be the toughest one yet. During that time period, Ken told me that it would just kill him if he knew that I was going to be hurting and alone after he passed. We looked at each other, tears in our eyes, and I told him that it looked like one way or another he was going to die, then. We both broke into laughter, and our laughter turned to crying as we hugged one another. We were both afraid and our fears brought us closer together. Ken was finally being intimate.

One night in November of 2008, Ken was at the computer in the dining room and I was cooking dinner. I had gone over to Ken's side to see what he had found on the computer. Very suddenly Ken looked up from the computer and asked if I had just seen what had crossed the dining room. I looked around very uneasy and asked him what he was talking about. He said, "You didn't see those three women?"

"What women?" I asked, goose bumps rising on my skin. Ken proceeded to tell me that he had been seeing these apparitions for the last month. I asked him if these manifestations were scary and he replied no, that he felt they meant him no harm. Knowing that he did not believe in ghosts, the supernatural, or paranormal occurrences, I asked him if seeing these women changed his mind, again he replied no. He explained it that reality, from what he had known it to be, was now changing. He gave the example of that salt now tasted like pepper. He offered no other explanation and did not seem overly concerned about these three women. Ken was moving closer to death, and was experiencing another dimension of being. My mother used to get visions, dreams, and feelings when death was getting close to our family. Many times Mom would smell roses right before we received a phone call from someone telling us a loved one had passed. Other times Mom would have a nightmare during which she would wake up screaming, where the person was visiting her in her dream. The next morning we would receive the news that person had died. Mom told me it was nothing to be afraid of, although she wished she did not have this "gift." I have witnessed to a lesser degree those same visions and dreams my mother had, and I believed what Ken was experiencing was somehow related.

Ken continued to lose ground, and soon he had no control over his bowel movements. We would wake up to the bed sheets and our bodies being completely covered in fecal waste and urine. I would shower off, and then get Ken to the shower while I changed the bedding and started another load in the washer. On bad nights this might happen twice. Ken was extremely embarrassed and discouraged; I told him to stop it, that shit happens, in our case it was just literally, trying to get some humor into the mix. Sometimes my humor would work, most often not. I told Ken it did not matter, I loved him, and I would do anything for him. He needed to trust me now more than ever, as I knew things would only get worse, and I wanted him to be at ease with me, no matter what. He would just look into my eyes and I would smile at him. Jessi would come back to Seattle from New Zealand, where she had been for the past eight months, attending college. She knew that Ken was bad and could not bear the thought of not seeing him one last time. This trip would be her goodbye to him and she stayed with us for approximately one month.

Soon Ken's bowel movements were mixed with a lot of blood, and that worried him, given that he had AIDS. I would be drenched in his blood and I assured him I was not at risk, I had survived being negative all these years; a little blood was not going to change that. I did tell him we needed to go to the doctor. I felt sure the cancer was back. Ken begged me not to take him back to the doctor; all they would do would be to place him back into the hospital. He won every time; I would clean him up and get us both back in bed, holding him until he stopped shaking from being cold from showering. I would have to leave Ken alone during the day and worried nonstop while at work. He was uneasy on his feet, he would have fewer accidents during

SEEING THROUGH THE GLASS DARKLY

the day, but they still happened. After work one day I found Ken still in bed, which was soaked with urine. I decided the time had come to take a leave of absence from work, as his time was nearing and I needed to be with him.

A few days later I was drying Ken off after I had given him a shower, and he asked me where John was. I thought I had not heard right, so I asked him what he had just said. Again he asked where John was. I told him that I was John and he replied that no, he meant "my John." My heart broke at that moment and I finished toweling him off, then got him to bed. They tell us that you cannot truly feel what a person has gone through in life until you have walked a mile in their shoes. That night I came to understand with much more clarity what people go through when they are dealing with loved ones who are suffering from dementia or Alzheimer's. I wondered if the cancer was metastasizing into his brain, or if this memory loss was because of the heavy medications he was taking. I called Ronnie, my main support during this time, and asked him to come from Columbus once again. Ronnie had been making frequent trips to Seattle and I told him we needed to get Ken to the doctor, and perhaps Ken would be more easily convinced if he was here to encourage Ken to get proactive. Ronnie once again came to Seattle and we were able to talk Ken into going to the doctor.

That afternoon, Ken, Ronnie and I sat in the examination room while the urologic oncologist told us he was sorry, but yes, the cancer had returned. The same cancer had invaded his urinary tract. The doctor immediately started to tell us our options, including having the urinary tract removed and having a reservoir on the outside of his body into which his ureters would void urine. Mind you, this was just months after a thirteen-hour surgery during which a blockage in his urethra had been cut out—scar tissue from the radiation treatment for the colon cancer. Ken stopped him, saying, "I don't want to talk about this anymore. I am done, I am tired, and I am through." The doctor expressed his understanding, and gently explained that doing nothing was a viable and understandable option. He added that, left untreated, the cancer would likely spread either to the base of his spine and hips, or to his lymph nodes. He then left us alone.

Ronnie and I were silent, and Ken started to speak, telling us that we should not be sad, that we had tried everything that was available and we had done our best. At that point, Ronnie and I started to cry with Ken joining in. Ken told us we would all get through this and he had not been given a death sentence—doctors were not gods and they did not have the final word on how this would play out.

Soon Ken had weakened to the point where he was no longer able to walk down the stairs to our bedroom, so I made the guest bedroom on the main floor our bedroom. There was a bathroom attached to this guest bedroom, so it would be perfect. Ken was in extreme pain from the cancer, which indeed had been found by scan to be in his spinal column, just weeks after the oncologist had predicted it. It was extremely painful and almost impossible for Ken to walk. I was of the opinion that I could get Ken walking again by having radiation treatment on his lumbar spine. I was fooling myself, but did not want to give in to this cancer. Even after his previous radiation treatment had destroyed intestinal and then urinary tract tissue, I was so taken by grief and not wanting to lose Ken that I would make a deal with the devil. I decided to get hospice involved, not from the perspective that Ken was dying, but just to help me out. Perhaps they could counsel me on better methods of taking care of him. Even trying to think in this manner, I was scared of hospice because of the stigma associated with that word. At this point, I was so afraid, and I needed to let Ronnie be aware of the current situation. I called Ronnie that afternoon and he was again in Seattle that next morning, his fifth trip from Columbus in eight months. Receiving the news that Ronnie was coming, I broke down and wept, so relieved that someone would be with me and perhaps calm me down as I was trying to calm Ken down.

The morning that Ronnie was coming, I woke up about 5:00 a.m. There in the doorway was a silhouette, the image of a man wearing a square hat and cape all in black, featureless. Although I could see

SEEING THROUGH THE GLASS DARKLY

no facial features, I felt that this thing, whatever it was, was not human, and was staring at us. I felt it was evil, maybe because of the black color, maybe because of the hat and cape, maybe because I was scared to death and this unknown had the advantage over me. Ken woke up, which was strange, because he was sleeping longer in the day and he asked who that was in the doorway. Startled that he was seeing this image also, I told him I did not know and asked him if he knew what it might be. Ken fell back to sleep immediately and I was alone with this image again. I closed my eyes and prayed whatever it was to please go away. I opened my eyes and it was still there, although it had appeared to fade a little. I closed my eyes again, and requested to God to please take this entity away. I kept my eyes closed for about five minutes and when I opened them, it was gone.

I slowly got out of bed and looked around the house, still not convinced this thing was gone. I even checked under the beds and in closets and when I did not find any trace of this creature I returned to Ken's bed and sat at his feet. I stayed with Ken until daylight broke, then while Ken slept I went downstairs to do some laundry and clean up some accidents Ken had. By this time, I was calming down from seeing this apparition and wondered if it had anything to do with the three women Ken had been seeing. Although I never saw the women, both Ken and I saw this other vision, and it more firmly made the argument that whatever we were witnessing was reality and not our imagination. I believed once again that Ken was experiencing another dimension of being and I, being so intertwined through love and caring for Ken, had been given an extraordinary gift of perhaps witnessing that threshold into death's door and another plane of existence. I felt once again that I was seeing through a glass darkly and was very unclear about what I had seen. I would not ridicule or scoff at this entity; I would be foolish to do so, as we humans know very little about death and what happens afterward. I was indeed frightened by what I had witnessed, but also felt very blessed that Ken saw what I had seen.

Others and I would again witness this unveiling of perhaps the threshold of Ken's entry into another beginning. Yet another door was opening for Ken—not a door where he would have to make another medical decision about his death, but a door that would perhaps reveal to Ken what was waiting on the other side of his approaching death.

CHAPTER **36**

Reunited

THE DAY THAT Ronnie arrived, a medical company was delivering the hospital bed, ordered by hospice care. I could see the fear and disbelief in his eyes. Ken's situation had deteriorated rapidly since Ronnie had seen his brother just a few weeks earlier. The time was arriving fast, even faster than I had imagined. That morning the hospice team came over and we talked of what they would be helping us with, how often, what we might expect, the care, and specifically controlling Ken's pain, which we were told was excruciating.

I had previously gotten hold of Ken's former partner, Christopher, who lived in Spain, and he would be arriving within the next few days. Ronnie called his family and told them they needed to come now, not to wait, as the outlook was getting much bleaker. Barb and Judy arrived the next day. As they entered the front door, I again saw all the hurt and dread in each of their faces. I felt such sadness for his family, especially Barb. I knew that I was losing my love, but she was losing a son. Her hurt was beyond my comprehension and my heart felt like it would implode ever trying to grasp what she was going through. Each of our hearts was breaking, and each of us could actually feel that physical pain. The next day Christopher arrived and I saw those same emotions all over again, this time mixed with much more disbelief than that shown by Ronnie just a few days earlier. I called Rachel and Kim and told them that I thought the end was getting very close, so Kim decided to come from Italy and see Ken one last time.

Those last few weeks of Ken's life were of course very sad, but at the same time I will always remember the support, prayers, encouragement, and love that were so abundant in our house. We each had our "household duties." Christopher was the chef. Each day he would go out shopping, then come home and make the most delicious meals. I was so depressed that I did not eat very much. I had lost twenty-five pounds, but what I did eat was amazing. Ken's family and I were in charge of changing Ken's positions in bed to try to avoid bedsores. Then we would all take turns reading or playing music that we thought Ken might enjoy. We were in the month of January, so the temperature was chilly, dipping in the 20s and 30s in the morning, but getting in the 50s and 60s by afternoon. Ken's hospital bed was right next to the fireplace, so that helped to keep him warm, as he seem to have the chills often. When we thought that it was warm enough, we would load Ken up in the wheelchair bundled up, and Judy and I would take him around the block for fresh air.

I remember the Sunday of January 25, 2009 we were watching the Screen Actors Guild Awards. Shane had joined us and Christopher had once again made an award-winning dinner and we all got our plates and crowded around Ken's bed as the show started. Ken loved films and the history of Hollywood. For the next two hours we made fun of everyone's dress or suit, their hair, their makeup, whatever we could make fun of, and we had a blast. Ken was not able to eat, as by this time he was starting to have trouble swallowing, but in our frivolous, indulgent conduct we had the best time, and I believe he did too, listening to all of the foolishness. I like to remember it as a last party for Ken—there was no crying that night, just laughter. Later that night, most of the neighbors came over to say their last goodbyes and there were tears then, but the love that Ken as an individual had elicited from our neighborhood was astounding. Dushka had to return back to Ohio that night to take care of their two daughters, but for that one special night we were all reunited as a family, and that

SEEING THROUGH THE GLASS DARKLY

was so good for everyone involved. Whenever one makes a memory, one is usually not aware they are doing so, which I guess is good. Otherwise, one might act differently and that memory might not be as special, or perhaps it would not end up being a memory at all. That night a memory was made for me, and when I think back to that night and remember all the faces there, surrounding Ken, I smile. What a precious gift memory is—one thing that death cannot destroy.

After everyone had retired for the night, I pushed the couch over by Ken's bed and stacked the cushions up so that I would be at the same level as Ken. This was my nightly ritual so that I could sleep right next to Ken and be there when he would wake up, need his bag changed, more pain medication, or if he just wanted to hold my hand. That night around 2:00 he woke up and we had a heart to heart. I did all the talking, as by this time Ken was too weak to vocalize anything. His eyes were so beautiful that night as I held his hand and told him he had been the best partner I could have ever wished for. Both of us were tearing up and I told him not to be concerned for me, that I would be okay, his family would take care of me and I would take care of them. I told him that I would take care of him the rest of my life if I could, but I knew he was in pain and that was so selfish of me to think that way. I told him that Sack of Shit (which Ken had for years jokingly referred to me as—the pretend brother of Sacajawea) had talked to the Almighty Father upstairs and my Father had assured me that He would take care of my love until one day when I would join him. Ken smiled at me and shook his head, squeezing my hand as tears rolled down my cheeks. Another memory made, so sweet and bitter.

That following Monday we witnessed what appeared to me as Ken seeing someone he knew. It was afternoon, and Ken, who had been sleeping more and more, woke up. As Ken looked around the living room his eyes seemed to focus on something that brought a smile to his face. His head turned as his eyes fixated on this person or thing he was seeing. His arms were outstretched as if he was trying to reach out and touch this object. Barb asked him what he was seeing, but he was too weak to answer and suddenly the smile left his face, he put his arms down, and his head fell back. Again I believe Ken was making contact with his new dimension where he would soon be. People might say it was the morphine, others might say it was the cancer; I believe all might be correct. But what I believe is that whatever vehicle was being used, whether it was the drugs, the cancer, or something we know nothing about, that method of transporting Ken closer to that new threshold was at work, and our witnessing should not be discounted because of disbelief of the unknown.

Ken passed away three days later on Wednesday, January 28, 2009 around 10:30 p.m. with Monkey by his side. I believe the last time he was awake was that Monday afternoon. His body was slowly shutting down and all we could do was to make sure he was not in pain. Ronnie and Kim were my main supports to make sure that I gave him his liquid morphine. Kim, being of clear mind, had to keep reminding me that even though Ken was perhaps unable to vocalize any pain he might be feeling, he would still feel the pain. Judy expressed concern to Ronnie that it seemed that I was giving Ken too much morphine, too often. Kim, Ronnie, and I were of the mind that Ken was very near death, and that efforts to ease his pain were paramount. We did not have enough morphine to kill him, or I might have considered that option. The last thing I would want for Ken would be pain—he had suffered enough, and for me, I believe there are things worse than death.

That night, everyone had gone to bed around 10:00. Kim and Shane had just left for the evening. Shane, before leaving, jokingly told Ken not to upstage his birthday, which was only two days away, by passing away before that time. I had not done my usual bed routine yet and Ronnie was fixing a late snack in the kitchen. I was watching Ken's breathing and wasn't quite sure if the pattern was changing or if it was my imagination. I called Ronnie into the living room and told him I thought something was different. We watched for a few minutes and Ken's breathing, although it had become more labored in the last few days, appeared to be normal for that time frame. I knew that I would not be sleeping that night because his breathing was much too labored to take a chance of falling asleep and Ken passing while I was sleeping—that was not going to happen. I continued to watch and his pattern changed again, this time much more abruptly. I ran into the kitchen and told Ronnie to get the family up, as I thought something was happening.

Ronnie ran downstairs to get Barb and Judy; Ronnie returned, and he sat to Ken's right, and I was seated to Ken's left. We held his hands and watched him slip away. Ronnie told me that just as Ken's breathing stopped, he firmly squeezed Ronnie's hand. Trying to hang on? Saying goodbye to us? Now that the time was here, all those years I had been preparing for this moment were not helping. I was paralyzed with grief, and angry that life had been so cruel and unfair to take Ken from me after we had finally gotten our life together right. I looked at my lover, just a shadow of the man I once knew, probably not weighing more than ninety pounds. His eyes had glazed over, but in my own mind they were still beautiful to me. I gently closed them as I kissed his eyelids, whispering in his ear that I loved him.

I called Kim and Shane and told them that Ken was gone. I told Shane just to come over tomorrow, but Kim immediately returned. All said their goodbyes, over a period of sixty minutes or so, and then I did my usual routine—pushing the sofa to his bed, stacking the cushions so I would be on the same level as Ken. I then got into bed, took Ken's hand into mine, kissed him on the forehead and told him I loved him once again, crying as I told him those words. I put down the side bars on the hospital bed and reached over and pulled Ken toward me, putting my head on his shoulder. Ken was now with that higher dancer we had discussed, and I would fall asleep with my lover for one last night.

CHAPTER **37**

Emptiness

THAT THURSDAY MORNING was surreal, very disorienting. I called Andy at work and told him that Ken had passed and asked if he would let the rest of my workplace know. Terri, my boss, had been very kind to Ken's family, at various times letting the Ross family stay at the hotel and sending over a basket of goodies to let us know the Rhody was thinking of us during the course of his illness. Ronnie had let the rest of the family know early that morning and, for the most part, all of us kept our minds busy with the mundane tasks that one does after a death. Kim was going back to Italy early that morning; tearfully we all said goodbye to her. Judy had requested if possible that we keep Ken with us till the afternoon and I told her that would be no problem, as we all wanted to hold on to Ken for as long as possible. The nurse from hospice was supposed to come over and take Ken's catheter out but never showed, so I took it out. I really did not want anyone touching my Ken anyway, except family, so I was glad to do this for Ken.

That afternoon after they picked up Ken's body, we made our way to the funeral home to sign the necessary papers. There would be no funeral ceremony, as Ken would be cremated, and I wanted to have a memorial when the weather was nicer, probably in July. We each stumbled through the day, each in our own thoughts and world. There were certain things of Ken's that his family wanted, so we spent the better part of Friday wrapping them for shipment back to Ohio.

◄ SEEING THROUGH THE GLASS DARKLY

That same day they picked up the hospital bed and Judy cleaned the front room and organized it back to its previous appearance. After her cleaning, I noticed a mark on the living room wooden floor. It was the mark where I slid the couch and the hospital bed together every night. I decided to leave it as a reminder to me of where my lover and I slept in our final days together. Friday night, Ronnie left for home. Judy and Shane accompanied me as I took Ronnie to the airport. We never made it to Sea-Tac Airport, because I was rear-ended near Qwest Field, so Ronnie had to catch a cab to the airport. The next day I took Barb and Judy to the airport for their flight home—no accidents this time. The only remaining one was Christopher, who returned to Spain on Monday.

That Sunday was probably the worst day of my life ever. Christopher was still in bed and I had gotten up early; daylight would be my salvation, darkness my slayer. It was a dreary, dismal, wet day in Seattle, but I had to go to Grocery Outlet on MLK Avenue and get copies of the *Seattle Times* for Ken's obituary. Ronnie had written the obituary and it was eloquent and complimentary, listing Ken's many accomplishments, focusing on the way his wit and humor could stop people in their tracks, and stating most importantly that he truly enjoyed his fellow beings. In short, his family would miss him and he was truly, deeply loved. I got to the grocery store where I purchased a dozen copies of the paper, one for me, the others for family members.

Once again, Marilyn my sister-in-law surprised me by being the first in my family to call and tell me how sorry she and Leland were upon hearing that my partner had passed away. She did not know Ken, but wanted me to know that she knew I was going through a rough time and just wanted me to know that she loved me. Again she touched my heart and surprised me at the same time. Patty also called and told me she knew what I was going through as she had lost her husband, Dick, a few years earlier. I knew also that Patty was sincere and she, as well, touched my heart. All the kids reached out to me as well and I could feel their presence in my heart through this sadness.

Monday I took Christopher to the airport, and then I stopped by

EMPTINESS

the hospital to tell them I would be returning to work the next day. As I got off the elevator, I saw Terri and immediately broke down. I knew coming back to work would be hard, but it was something I knew would be better for me than just staying at home feeling miserable. At least I would be at work feeling miserable, receiving support, and making money.

The restaurant customer base was made up of many groups: doctors and nurses, the neighborhood's elderly, other medical organizations' staff, patients and patients' families, and different church organizations on the Hill. My second day back at work, one of my last tables consisted of this last group—churchgoers. It was a woman and a man. The man was your typical suit and tie, religious-looking fellow. The woman was much more picturesque, like a southern belle right out of a southern woman's magazine. This woman I would say was right around fifty, beautiful Botox face, bottle-blonde hair that was big—so big I am sure she did feel closer to God—jewelry that would have made even Jezebel envious, and breasts that were straining beneath her tightly fitted blouse, so perky, one would have to wonder if she were truly born with them. I surmised they were not from the Catholic faith, because although the Catholics are many things, they would not have been this hurtful toward me. I would have to say I think I knew all of the Catholics that patronized the restaurant and they, in turn, had come to know me over the fourteen years that I had worked at the Rhododendron. I think without exception I liked all of them, as they represented to me a great people.

This woman and man were having a conversation, and although we servers do not eavesdrop on private conversations, the Rhody, being a public place without walls, we hear a lot. Their conversation centered on homosexuality and woe to those who were practicing this abomination, because it would truly mean an ill omen on their souls. I listened at length. To the point: If what they were saying was true, Ken and I would never even have the chance of seeing each other again, if there was such a thing as an afterlife. I gave this couple their check and kept thinking about what they had said. I started to

SEEING THROUGH THE GLASS DARKLY

analyze the possibility of the "what ifs." I began to panic. I cashed out as fast as I could and caught the bus home. Once inside I called Celia, a good friend of Ken's, and was crying uncontrollably into the phone, trying to tell her what had just happened. Having a hard time comprehending the message I was trying to relay to her about Ken's and my condemned souls to eternal hell fire, she rushed over to my place right away. As soon as she got there, I started to babble all over again, relating to her the conversation I had heard from these two zealots. I told her that as much as it hurt to lose Ken, the thought of possibly never having the chance to see him again was overwhelming and I could not take that kind of torture. I told her if this was truly God, I wanted no part of Him—this was not love, this was hate and He was a despicable God, if He was a god at all.

Celia told me that she couldn't believe I had even listened to this crap. She believed that this "possible higher being" was love, and if what these people were saying was accurate, then truly God was not love and she wanted no part of Him either. But she did not believe this was the truth, and she believed these people were in error; they had likely misunderstood the Bible and were utterly without compassion. As she continued to speak, I began to calm down and my hysteria slowly diminished. I thanked her for coming over and rescuing me before I went to pick up Ken's ashes that day. Celia offered to accompany me to the funeral home and I gladly accepted. We went and picked up Ken, who weighed a whopping eight pounds, and then went to my Starbucks on Capitol Hill, where again she calmed me down and gave me assurance those religious crazies were just that: crazy.

That night I would be with my love once again, although I would not tell anyone. I did not believe that people would see things quite the way I saw them. I now had Ken's ashes and although they were cremains, they were his cremains; his DNA was still there. They were given to me in a plastic sack contained further in a rectangular plastic container and contained one more time in a cloth sack. I went to bed that night holding Ken and Monkey to my chest, crying as I fell asleep, hoping I would dream about Ken and at least be reunited with him in my dream world. Those dreams never came until almost eighteen months had passed; I would console myself by holding Ken and Monkey each night as I fell asleep. This I know is not for everyone, but it was my way of healing, and it worked.

The next several months I kept busy doing odd jobs around the house—those little "touch-ups" Ken and I had always talked about doing but never did. The list was quite long, so it kept me busy. Also, there was much cleaning to do after Ken had passed. His health issues had created the need to do a very thorough house cleaning, which took almost a month to complete. The hardest room was the laundry room, where I had spent so many hours. Just being in that room brought back so many memories, all of them sad. Along with doing these little jobs, I also had the responsibilities of those jobs that Ken had been responsible for. These jobs created anxiety for me as well as sadness. I had never thanked Ken for doing everything that he did around the house; I just took it for granted. The first week of his passing, I had to take the car in for servicing and, riding the bus back home, I realized how much Ken had done for us, and again I was mad at myself for not taking the time to thank him—or for that matter even to realize the extent of what he did. I would never have that chance to tell him. I must not make that same mistake with other loved ones. I must tell them how much they are appreciated. This point would be drilled further into my consciousness as I sat in the stylist's chair a few weeks later, tears streaming down my cheeks, getting my hair cut by someone other than Ken for the first time in over a decade.

In the area of our finances, Ken had been very careful to make sure any and all accounts would be transferred over to me with little or no effort on my part. I went to tell his bank, where he had a private account, that he had passed. Before doing so, though, I asked the officer if I could leave his account open as there would still be a few more payments made from this account. She assured me they would leave the account open so these bills would get paid. Just as soon as I gave them Ken's name, they closed the account immediately. I started crying, asking why they had lied to me. She told me it was just the law; they had no choice, even though she had made that choice by lying to me. She could have told me what would happen and just to come back after the bills were paid. I did not want the monies that were given to me that night, but the bank thought that more important than having any compassion for me. I learned that most businesses did not have a heart—they were uncaring, and they would give me their lip service, their empty words of condolence, but it was just business to them. From his cell phone service to his gym membership, they did not care that he had died; he had signed up for a two-year service agreement and they were not going to let him out of the agreement just because he had died Who are these morons? I finally got everything straightened out, except for his cell phone bill. This major global telecommunications company initiated a collection agency to collect the payment they thought was owed them. I will never have them as my carrier and they truly are a company that is without heart.

The exception was TD Ameritrade. I called the Omaha headquarters to get the paperwork started, and in the course of taking care of this business I had to talk to three different people. Every single one of these workers for TD Ameritrade would politely stop me from talking and to start out the conversation with me they said they needed to express their sympathy for my loss. One guy told me he did not know how I was even able to talk to him after my loss. He told me that if he lost his wife he would be a total mess. I told him that it was my partner I had lost and he told me, "Mr. Garlick it doesn't matter if that love was between two men, two women, or a man and woman, love is love and again I am so sorry you have to go through this." Each one of those workers made me cry and I will always be loyal to TD Ameritrade. They showed me heart and have always protected my interests, and now they were showing me the human side of their company.

I was extremely depressed after Ken's passing, so I made an appointment to see my doctor. My doctor at Virginia Mason was extremely understanding and very compassionate. He told me that losing one's spouse or partner was probably one of the hardest things a person would ever have to endure. Perhaps losing one's child might be the most difficult. I informed him that I was thinking a lot about suicide those days, and had even put a butcher knife to my stomach and drawn blood. I did not want to put my family through the agony of another death, so I stopped. I did ask him if he would do some blood work on me, explaining about being covered in Ken's blood during his last months and perhaps if life was kind I might have contracted HIV through Ken. If that was true, I would not want treatment, I just wanted to die. My doctor just looked at me, not speaking, his eyes wide with what I had just said, and I started to cry. This doctor took the time to speak to me, prescribe the necessary medications, and gave me his personal cell number. My doctor even started showing up at the restaurant— coincidence? Probably not. I was lucky to have such a caring doctor, and Virginia Mason was lucky to have such a person on their payroll.

CHAPTER **38**

Final Goodbye

SPRINGTIME CAME EARLY that year and as the tulips began to emerge from the thawing ground, I remembered I had hoped Ken would be around for one more season. The previous year I had planted close to one thousand red tulips and they were spectacular. This year would prove to be even more spectacular and I had wanted Ken to see the fruits of our labor just one more time. I was angry that our life had worked out the way it did. All those years we had wasted by not communicating effectively, or letting fear take the upper hand, preventing us from finding a true happiness with each other. As a way of combating that anger I found that working in the yard was very healing for me, and it was my meditation. I would get lost in nature and all that was around me. Our yard was so amazing with many different varieties of plants, flowers, and trees. It was my goal to make the yard the best in show for Ken's memorial. I knew that I wanted the memorial at our house and the yard would be the crowning jewel in honoring his memory. So I kept myself very busy in preparing for his memorial.

Jessi had returned from New Zealand again, as she was having a very hard time with Ken's passing. That summer I will always remember Jessi and Shane being over at my house constantly. I know they were worried about me and did not want me to be alone. I gave in to their concerns and accepted their worries for me with an open door. Their company was actually nice and it took my mind off of the

FINAL GOODBYE

loneliness and pain that were very much constant in my life. To help with the pain and depression, I continued my visits to the doctor. Besides being extremely depressed, almost suicidal, I had such low levels of energy. My doctor helped by supplying me with antidepressants, which I took for almost a year before getting off of them. The medication, along with a few sessions with a psychiatrist, helped my anxiety and depression greatly.

To get ready for Ken's memorial, I started collecting pictures of various times in Ken's life; these would be used to make a DVD memorial accompanied by music that Ken liked or that meant something in our relationship. I hired a classical trio consisting of two violins and a cello, so there would be live classical music during the entire evening. A catered buffet from my workplace would be provided free of charge and the coffee would be provided free of charge from the Starbucks on Olive Way. Three of the baristas from this Starbucks would be serving the guests. I contacted a party supply company for the tables, chairs, and tablecloths. I typed up a program for the guests to follow as they watched the DVD that would be running constantly in the living room. The memorial was held on Saturday, July 25, 2009. Even though it had been six months since Ken had passed away, the memorial was attended by more than eighty people. From Ken's family, Ronnie, Dushka, and their two daughters attended, as well as Barb and Judy. The weather cooperated nicely, and I was very touched by the attendance and the kind words that the guests had for Ken. We gave him a great sendoff, and the tribute we all paid to his memory was most fitting for the life Ken had lived.

Now that the memorial was over, I was faced with dealing with the loss of Ken all over again. Having been so occupied with planning his memorial had kept my mind from really grasping the reality that Ken was truly gone and would never return. In a strange way, I had kept Ken alive through this memorial service, and I did not let reality spoil that fantasy world I had created in my mind. Yes, I knew Ken was dead, but he was still living daily with me while I planned his "goodbye." I suddenly realized that I had not said my goodbye to my

◄ SEEING THROUGH THE GLASS DARKLY

love, that I was waiting as long as I could until I had to say that word that was so final. So the time had come that Saturday night, and now I would need to find a more permanent solution for dealing with my loss. My lover was gone.

CHAPTER **39**

The Autumn of 2009

THE CHILL OF autumn came early to the Northwest, just as springtime had. I welcomed the crispness in the air, and it took me back to the last year when Ken and I were still able to take walks around the block in our pajamas. I would sit on the porch, many times until dusk, just going through the memories in my mind, all the time wishing there was some way that I could go back just one more time. Jessi had returned to New Zealand and Shane's visits were getting less frequent. I would do fine during the weekdays. I had my work and going to the gym afterwards. After arriving home I would often escape the emptiness of the house by going to Starbucks and reading or listening to music. I started to read books written by the Dalai Lama. This interest in the Dalai Lama was triggered by a sexual encounter that I had with a handsome man who was interested in the Buddhist faith. This man was struggling with various addictions and proved not to be very reliable in companionship, but I will be forever grateful to him for introducing me to the great writings of this man. This man also taught me that we as humans are uniquely connected through our sadness and trials in life. The Dalai Lama's handbooks for living, his viewpoints, and teachings brought me much peace and inspiration. Although I was not a Buddhist, I admired the Dalai Lama for being so down to earth. He covered everyday topics with such ease and grace, unlike many of our American pastors and priests, who sprinkled their

SEEING THROUGH THE GLASS DARKLY

teachings with dogma and personal prejudices without much thought or reason. His books gave me calm in my life that I had not had for many years. I started to see things differently and I started to see Ken's passing in a new light, a light that gave me a little hope where before there was only darkness.

The Dalai Lama's teachings even affected me at the bus stop. I had just gotten off work one afternoon and was waiting at the bus stop to go home. At this bus stop was this developmentally disabled woman, probably in her mid-twenties. I had seen this young woman with her mother in the restaurant several times over the years. This woman approached me and started a conversation with me, asking how I was. I politely responded that I was doing well, but inwardly I was perturbed that this woman was speaking to me. I did not feel like speaking to anyone, and just wanted to get home and then probably go to Starbucks. Then the teachings of the Dalai Lama came to mind and I asked WWKD (What would Ken do?). Ken would engage this woman, like he had engaged the schizophrenic at Starbucks. So, although I did not really want to have a conversation with this woman, I forced myself to do so. For the next ten minutes I talked with this woman and giving my time and energy to her made me feel better. When the bus arrived we said our goodbyes, and got on the bus and went to our separate seats. I smiled as I looked across the aisle at this woman and I patted myself on the back. Ken would have been proud of me; the Dalai Lama would have been proud of me—shit, I was proud of me.

The weekends were a different story. Whereas during the weekdays, I had structure and a schedule to my life, when the weekend came I was on my own. The weekend started Friday night. I was so afraid of being alone in the stillness of the house, and as a result my anxiety would skyrocket. So every Friday night I would schedule my weekly massage session and increase it to ninety minutes instead of just sixty. That would get me through the first half of the night. Then sometimes I would go to Starbucks as I usually did on weeknights. But Friday nights were not the same there as they were on the weekdays.

THE AUTUMN OF 2009

The crowd was different and the feel was also different; I did not enjoy it there on Fridays, and would feel even more alone than if I had just stayed home.

I needed someone to be around. It didn't matter who—just someone I could talk to and feel their presence to take my mind off of this terrible feeling of being alone. I wanted to feel a warm body, to touch and be touched. I would go on Craigslist, a gay chat line, or a gay hookup site. Sex was not the goal here, but it was usually the goal of most of the other guys that were online. That was fine, and I certainly was not one to judge anyone, and I certainly wasn't going to throw stones. I would search until I felt reasonably comfortable with the guy that I would be hooking up with. I had heard and read of the horror stories of people getting killed through Craigslist and I was going to make sure that I would not be the next headline. I would ask enough questions and make sure that the questions I was asking would point out whether they were not from the area and were probably just out for the weekend and wanting to have some quality gay-bashing time. Luckily I never came across such people. Instead, I came across people who were also lonely and alone, much as I was. Each had his own story, and we helped each other out of whatever desperation and hopelessness we were feeling that night. I met many sweet guys during the next few months and it gave me a new perspective on how I viewed these hookup sites; I became less judgmental. The aphorism of "one cannot experience what his brother or sister is experiencing until you have walked a mile in their shoes" was so applicable here. I am glad to have walked this particular mile; it made me a better person. Sometimes there would be no hookup. Instead, I would chat with the other person for a few hours until I was tired enough to be able to fall asleep after crawling into my bed and could avoid the stillness of the first night of the weekend.

Sometimes Louis, a good friend, would be able to talk me into going to the Cuff or some other gay club on a Saturday night. Louis knew I loved to dance, so he would use that angle to get me out the door. I would go with him, but usually I would just not be in the mood, or there would be a bitter queen who would take offense because I was not in a talking mood. As I believe to be the norm, these bitter queens were probably insecure and did not think for a second that it was not about them. I would politely tell them no or try to excuse myself and they would counter with a snide remark. I had no patience with their self-centeredness, and would usually leave the club upset, wondering what was wrong with the gay community. Our community, it seemed, could judge very harshly, especially when situations or ideas did not fit into "their norm." And yet, we are so vocal when we as a group perceive that we are judged unfairly. I wondered if we really did not see the irony.

So with those few incidents I was inclined to shy away from the clubs. I would just peruse the online sites. One such time I came across this guy I had talked to about three other times. We had tried getting together, but he lived by Northgate and I lived in the Central District, so for each of us, it was not the most convenient of hookups. So I skipped over his profile and went searching elsewhere. I would come back to his name and picture periodically and think perhaps I should just bite the bullet and meet him at his place. After all, he was closer to my age—I was guessing eight to ten years younger than I—was very handsome, had a great smile, and I loved his eyes. His eyes were very beautiful, with that blue/hazel shade that changed with the surroundings. His conversations were polite and he seemed nice, at least online. I started talking to him and we ended up making a date for that Friday night. His name was Clayton and I told him that sex would be okay, but that it was more than that for me. I wanted to be with someone, perhaps watch a movie together. I could bring Chinese food over and I wanted to stay the night and just be close to someone. I did not tell him that I had lost Ken, as I did not want him feeling sorry for me or worse yet, thinking I was some sort of weirdo. He agreed to the date and I waited for Friday night to come.

Friday came and I got off work and did my usual schedule of going to the gym, then an earlier massage appointment, after which I showered and went to pick up the Chinese takeout that I had ordered.

THE AUTUMN OF 2009

We were going to meet up at 8:00 and driving there, I wondered what this guy would be like. The other guys I had been with had eased the loneliness, but there was no connection for me. We all had our pain and our stories, but it seemed that most of the guys were too consumed with their own problems to deal with mine. I certainly did not want to take on any added burdens and problems of their indiscriminate choices, which ran the gauntlet from sex, drugs, and alcohol, to domestic violence. I did not judge these men—I did not know their full stories—but at the same time, I did not want to be a part of their story. I was still writing my own, and I was not ambidextrous.

I arrived at Clayton's right before 8:00 and entered the apartment complex. I found my way to his apartment and knocked on his door, wondering if the Clayton who was on the internet would look like the Clayton who would be answering the door. The door opened and his gorgeous eyes met mine, along with everything else I had seen on my computer screen. I smiled; Clayton asked me how I was doing and I replied: "My day just got a lot better." Not a bad line if I do say so myself. He smiled bigger and invited me in.

That night we had sex, which was amazing; we had Chinese, which was good, watched a movie while we cuddled, and then spent the night together, which was so comforting. We both slept well, did not suffer the awkwardness of having a stranger in bed, and we molded into each other's body, which was very nice and sweet. Clayton was a pretty boy, a down on the farm boy, not the macho type that Ken had been. He had this sweetness about him that put me at ease and was appealing. Clayton had to go to work by 11:00, so I left around 10:00, and told him I would call and plan something for the next weekend. I did call, but it was not for the next weekend; I bumped up the schedule so we would get together in a few days. Clayton was okay with that, and soon we were seeing each other almost every night.

Clayton came into my life at the exact time I needed him. He was so patient and saintly with me, and dealt with my depression from having lost Ken. At the time we met, Lady Antebellum's hit song

SEEING THROUGH THE GLASS DARKLY

"Need You Now" was on the air constantly. It seemed like every time we would get into the car, this song would be on. This song, like so many other things in our relationship, seemed like a bridge of sorts. Lady Antebellum sings of being drunk and vowing not to call her lover, but gives in and calls anyway. Years ago, when Ken was in Germany, he had gotten drunk and he woke me up with a telephone call at 1:30 in the morning (the time in the song was 1:15 a.m.). Ken told me he was lonely and he just wanted to hear my voice. This song also asks the question of whether the thought of her ever crossed her lover's mind. I had often wondered where Ken might be and if I ever was in his thoughts. Needless to say, "Need You Now" became our song and it will always have a very special and tender spot in my heart. For almost the first year, when hearing this song, I would cry. Clayton would just touch me and smile.

There were many other bridges in our developing relationship. At times it would almost be scary, the similarities between Clayton and Ken. Both loved spicy foods. Both knew their cars and the history of the automobile industry. Both were handy around the house. Both could find their way anywhere without a compass. Both were computer-savvy. Many times Clayton would say something and I would stop him, asking him to repeat what he had just said. With that questioning face he would do as I requested, and sometimes I would be silent, just thinking of the past. The phrase or wording that Clayton would have just vocalized would be almost the exact wording Ken had used in the past. Sometimes these incidents would almost make be believe in reincarnation. Ken perhaps had come back to me via Clayton.

There were many differences to set the two men apart also. These differences were much like the love that I had for each of them. After I lost Ken, this woman who was on her third marriage, twice a widow, came into the Rhododendron. This woman told me that she felt that I was very loving and caring, evident by the way I had listened to her story, and felt I genuinely knew and felt the pain that people were going through. She said in recognizing this capacity for love and caring in me, she felt certain that I would find another love. She said it would be different, not the same as the first, but still special in its own way. At the time, I thought this woman was just trying to cheer me up, but her words rang true—I did find another love, and this love for Clayton was indeed different from my love for Ken. I do not try to differentiate between the two loves. One is not greater or lesser than the other, but still they are different. People have asked me to explain—I cannot, will not. For me, trying to perceive the difference in or between the two only makes them less than what they truly are.

I knew that Clayton was a good man and of good heart one day when I came home from work. Clayton had stayed over at my place that night because he had the next day off and he could take his leisure in doing whatever he cared to do—no need to worry about getting to work. I had to leave for work at 5:30, so Clayton would be making the bed. I guess this was the first time that Clayton was the latter one up, or perhaps we'd both had the same days off before that time. I came home finding that Clayton had gone back to his apartment, and I proceeded to go downstairs. I got to my bedroom, where I stopped and looked at the bed neatly made…my tears started forming. I was not crying because Clayton had made the bed; I was crying because of how he made the bed. As I confessed, after Ken's passing I would sleep with Ken's ashes and Monkey—both gave me comfort and peace. I had never talked about this with Clayton but he picked up on it. He never really knew what this cloth bag contained, but he surmised it might be Ken. All Clayton knew was this item must be important to me and he was not going to question my actions. He had seen me take it out of the bed before we retired for the night and then make the bed with Monkey and this cloth sack included in the make-up. Seeing the bed made up with Monkey and Ken made for healing in my heart and a place in my heart for Clayton. This simple act was so loving and caring, and Clayton did not even question me about it. I was taken aback by the thoughtfulness of his deed. I took both Ken and Monkey in my arms and started sobbing. Something was telling me a step was coming and soon I would be ready to take that step.

SEEING THROUGH THE GLASS DARKLY

Clayton was helping me with his love and patience. Life was being good to me once more. People say one is fortunate when one can find someone who loves you in life. I was fortunate two times—I had once again found my heart's love, and his name was Clayton.

CHAPTER **40**

Thanks for the Trips, Ken

AFTER KEN PASSED, he had many travel miles on his credit card. I knew that if the credit card company found out he had died, these miles would vanish. When Shelly had passed away she had willed her travel miles over to Ken, but the company would not honor her wishes and her miles disappeared. I was going to make sure that did not happen here. Ken had left me all the usernames and passwords for all of his accounts; all I had to do were keep the account current, pay the bill, and book my travel plans right away. The first trip I booked was for a round-trip vacation to Italy to see Kim and Rachel. That trip I booked for around three months out. The next trip I would book would be to Palm Springs, California. Ken and I had vacationed frequently in Palm Springs, so I thought it would be most fitting. I booked this trip one year in advance for February of 2010. I thought by then, I might be feeling better and less sad about his death. These two trips almost did away with all the points.

The trip to Italy was okay; the best part was being with the girls and having their support. Going to Europe was not a big thing for me; it was mainly about getting away and trying to clear my head and heart of this great loss I had suffered. Kim and Rachel were sweet, caring, and understanding, just what I needed most at that time.

When it came time for the trip to Palm Springs, Andy asked me if I was going to look at real estate while down there. I asked him

SEEING THROUGH THE GLASS DARKLY

why would I look at houses—I had one in Seattle. He proceeded to tell me that one could get a house in California very cheaply. I went home that night and looked at what was selling around Palm Springs; I called Clayton up and told him to also look. I honestly thought there was something the listings were not telling us, because these prices were much too low, or something had to be wrong with these houses. Over the next few weeks, Clayton and I continued to look at the housing market in Palm Springs and one day I came home with a question for Clayton. I asked him if he had ever considered living in California, and whether he had any opinions about the state. Immediately Clayton told me he would go with me in a heartbeat to Palm Springs. He was ready now. Almost instantly he apologized for assuming that I would want him to move with me to California. The look on his face was so sweet, and once again he melted my heart—he was so good to me. Of course I wanted him to go with me, even if we were acting like two lesbians and couldn't wait to load the trailer for that first date. It had been only a few months, but this guy was very special. I asked Clayton if he could get some time off to go with me to Palm Springs, and while there we could look at some houses for fun, if nothing else.

I had been told when Ken passed not to make any major decisions for at least a year, and I had kept to that time frame. It had been a year now, and I knew that if I was going to be serious about perhaps making a life with Clayton, that we would have to have a new start, away from Seattle and away from this sadness of not being able to complete my life with Ken. I thought I would never sell the house that Ken and I had bought together, but the memories, albeit many of them happy, included so many that were bittersweet, and it would not be fair to Clayton. Clayton got the time off and we planned our first trip together, much like Ken and I had done so many years before.

CHAPTER 41

Off to a New Beginning

WHEN LANDING IN Palm Springs that February, it was much the same as landing on a tropical island for us. The weather, in the 80s, was a dramatic change from the damp and cold of Seattle. I stepped off the plane to be greeted by a rush of warm desert air; it was good to be back in Palm Springs.

Before leaving Seattle, we had gotten in touch with Gregory, a realtor in Palm Springs. We had provided Gregory with a list of needs, wants, likes, and dislikes in what we were looking for in a home. We told him we would be in the area for just a few days and, if possible, we would like to schedule a day viewing property around the Coachella Valley, particular in Palm Springs Proper. Gregory picked us up the next day at our hotel and he had over twenty listings to show us. He was very organized, starting in Palm Springs, then gradually heading east in the valley. The showings that day were very fun and opened our eyes to a possible different kind of life in sunny California. California real estate had been hit hard and homes were at a discount especially, if you could offer a cash buy. I saw one home in particular that I really liked and I put an offer on it that night. Fortunately, there was another buyer who had put an offer on the same house a few hours before I did, and that offer was taken. I use the word "fortunately," as the house that we finally got was far better in all aspects than this one.

SEEING THROUGH THE GLASS DARKLY

Clayton did not have as many days as I did for Palm Springs, so he headed back to Seattle while I stayed in Palm Springs for three more days. I looked at a few more houses, but found nothing that really caught my attention. So I headed back to Seattle at the end of the weekend and after arriving back home put my house on the market.

My home had lost approximately 15% in resale value since I had purchased it three years ago, but considering what I would be getting in Palm Springs, I would be coming out way ahead. The selling process was extremely difficult. Having a strong sentimental attachment to my home made it difficult to start with, and coupled with the fact that we were dealing with arduous people, it did not make for anyone being happy. Since the market had downturned, people assumed that all sellers were desperate and would do about anything to sell their place. My house had strong bones and everything had been repaired or replaced, so anything they had to complain about was on a personal level. I cannot even use the word cosmetic, as the house was appealing, just not everyone's taste. I soon tired of trying to appease everyone and finally was of the opinion if they wanted something different, they could change it after they purchased it. I learned that the majority of buyers had no imagination unless every detail was laid out in front of them. I grew tired of spending money trying to give each buyer the "look" they were wanting, and grew annoyed. I believe my realtor picked up on this, as I was receiving far fewer change requests on the house and I am sure my message was passed on to any prospective buyers. After about forty-five days we had an offer on the house and after a nickel and diming process on the buyer's part, we had an agreement. The house would be closing June 17, 2010.

Prior to the sale of my home in Seattle, we had put an offer on a Spanish-style house in Palm Springs, the sale of which was contingent on the sale of my home in Seattle. Just to be ahead of the ball game, I had sent Clayton back down to Palm Springs for the inspection of this house. This home also had strong bones, and although every detail was not laid out for Clayton and me, we had enough foresight to envision how to make this house our home. Now that we had a strong offer on the house in Seattle, we could go forward with the home in Palm Springs. Since the groundwork had been nearly completed on this sale, about the only thing to do was the signing of the papers. This house would be closing June 18, 2010.

The final process would be the packing of our belongings. Clayton had already packed his possessions and the majority of his items were in storage. To save money, Clayton had moved in with me for the last two months while we waited for the houses to close escrow; the money saved could be better spent on our move to California. In the process of once again packing to move to another house, my mind went back three years earlier. Then I had been packing up my condo to start a new life with Ken. I was so excited that at last Ken had committed to moving in with me. Now three years had passed and Ken was gone, and yet another wonderful man had entered my life. This time Clayton, much like I had been three years earlier, was the one that was so excited to be going back to southern California that he had been missing for years. I, much like Ken three years earlier, was the more sedate one, more cautious, wondering where this new adventure would take us.

I looked around the house, boxes and clutter everywhere, memories coming almost literally out of the woodwork. I stopped packing and just sat there, thinking, reflecting on my life and wondering how in the world I had gotten to this place. For a brief period I just wanted to sit there and not have to think. I was tired of change, as it had come so often in my life, and although change had worked out for my good, it was nevertheless always demanding and tiring.

My thoughts went to my mom and dad and I wondered if they had gone through similar experiences in their life that I did not know about, and I wondered if I was more like them than I let myself believe. I reflected on my siblings and wished I had been closer to them growing up. I thought about my nieces and nephews whom I had helped raise and hoped I had not screwed their lives up too much with my imperfect parenting skills. The mistakes I did make raising

SEEING THROUGH THE GLASS DARKLY

them, I hoped they would forgive me; I had been able to keep them together as a family, at least. Then my reminiscences skipped to Mary, and how she would have loved to experience these changes that were happening in my life. Then my mind went to Ken and Clayton. Two handsome men had chosen me, Spud, pimple boy. I couldn't be much luckier than that. For my life experiences and for the person I grew to be, I believed I owed much thanks to certain people in my life.

I silently thanked my classmates for being so cruel to me; they made me a much better person than I would have been without their cruel jokes, names, and bullying. Without realizing it, my classmates gave me the gift of caring for others by not caring about me. Without realizing it, my classmates gave me the gift of empathy by detaching their own selves from feeling anything around them except perhaps hatred for their selves and others. Without realizing it, my classmates gave me the last laugh by letting me experience my first loss: that of being ostracized by my peers. Without realizing it, my classmates gave me the greatest gift of all: my ability to love fueled by their hatred for me. I was indeed a kinder, gentler, more loving—and yes, stronger—person because of them, and for that I was thankful.

The next morning Clayton and I, too excited to sleep would rise at 3:00 to start our life anew in the desert. We were off to our own new beginning, and what we would make of it would be determined only by us. Together we would find our own niche in life, we would learn from and teach each other, and together we would strive to find happiness together.

The Killers asked in the song "Human," *Are we human or are we dancer?* The reference of the lyric is widely believed, according to interviews with Brandon Flowers, to come from American gonzo journalist Hunter S. Thompson, who criticized Americans for their loss of individuality and emotion. Thompson asserted that America was raising a "generation of dancers," implicating a societal movement toward blindly following choreographed and mindless behaviors—stay in line and do not dare miss a step. The expression of individuality and emotion are uniquely human. A lack of emotion and individuality, like a sheep being herded as one among a flock, is uniquely inhuman. They are "dancer," referred to by Thompson as a quality of existence and not a verb or noun. The bullies that I have made reference to in this book were "dancer," being choreographed by an audience of peers and teachers who were probably bullied as well, yet who condoned their actions by keeping silent or outwardly praising them for their actions. The religious couple at the Rhody, spewing anti-gay biblically-laced carbon copies of what they had been taught, was "dancer." And yet as ironic as life can be, these bullies probably have the least amount of power among us. These bullies, I believe, had such a desire to be popular and liked by their jury of equals that they allowed others to control their actions, thoughts, and hearts without realizing how much of their individuality they were sacrificing. So, the question posed by Brandon Flowers cannot be answered by forced choice. Some of us are "human," and others "dancer."

    I never followed, although I was traumatized by not following the scripted choreography, injured by stepping out of line with the dance, anxious and depressed at various stages in my life, but I never held hate in my heart, even when I wanted so badly to hate. As in the Killer's song, I was brought up to my own table of surrender, thanks in large part to my classmates and to my first love, Ken. They have made me a better person, each in dramatically different ways, and I have been able to learn to cut the cord in this life with clear heart.

    No longer does death have the sting it once had. I have come to sincerely appreciate that childhood teaching from my mother—that death is a part of the circle of life, and without it there can be no rebirth, no new beginnings. I have come to understand there are far worse things in life than death. So I will wave goodbye to you my readers and I will wish myself well and try to forgive myself for those mistakes I have made in this life, even though at times that is hard for me to do. I thank you for sharing my story, that of another human. So deeply in love again, the desert calls out. No apparitions. No visions.

SEEING THROUGH THE GLASS DARKLY

No mirages. Awaiting is a house that will become a lovely home in which to listen, to love, to grow new gardens, and to find firm footing on new land. I am seeing through my glass a little less darkly, no reservations needed.

CPSIA information can be obtained at www.ICGtesting.com
Printed in the USA
LVOW08s1739100813

347214LV00003B/174/P